THIS IS

RE!

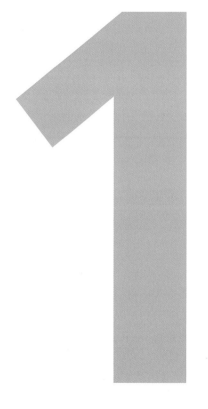

HODDER
EDUCATION
AN HACHETTE UK COMPANY

Notes
The terms BCE (Before Common Era) and CE (Common Era) have been used throughout. Transliteration of Hindi and Buddhist words follows the QCA-recommended spellings. Buddhist words are all from Pali, except Nirvana.
Words printed in SMALL CAPITALS (first mention only) are defined in the Glossary on pages 116–118.

© Cath Large 2002

First published 2002
by Hodder Education, an Hachette UK company
338 Euston Road
London NW1 3BH

Reprinted 2003, 2004 (twice), 2005, 2006, 2007, 2008, 2010

Although every effort has been made to ensure that website addresses are correct at the time of going to press, Hodder Education cannot be held responsible for the content of any website mentioned in this book.

Layouts by Liz Rowe
Artwork by Oxford Designers and Illustrators Ltd
Cover design by John Townson/Creation
Typeset in 13/14pt Goudy by Wearset Ltd, Boldon, Tyne and Wear
Printed and bound in Italy

A CIP catalogue record for this book is available from the British Library.

ISBN 978 0 719 57439 9
Teacher's Book ISBN 978 0 719 57520 4

THIS IS
RE!

CATH LARGE

General consultant Alan Brine
County General Inspector RE, Hampshire

1

HODDER
EDUCATION

Contents

Final task	Key words	ICT opportunities	QCA links
• Design and make a bookmark	• Belief • Opinion • Question • Religion • Experience • Argument • Atheist • Agnostic	• Make a bookmark using word processing package	✓✓7A Where do we look for God?
• Research and write a report on worship for a children's TV news programme	• Mandir • Brahman • Murti • Ritual • Puja	• Research worship using CD-ROMs or the internet • Prepare survey on worship and use database to sort information	✓8C Beliefs and practice (generic) ✓8E A visit to a place of worship (generic)
• Design a poster to illustrate how the Christian story is relevant in the world today	• New Testament • Creation • Incarnation • Crucifixion • Resurrection	• Fax or e-mail Christian schools and communities and ask what the story means to them	✓8A What does Jesus' incarnation mean for Christians today? ✓8B What does the resurrection of Jesus mean for Christians today?
• Design a poster with words and pictures to summarise Christian ideas about justice	• Justice • Reconciliation • Neighbour	• Research Christian response to injustice, referring to websites of organisations • Record role play	✓✓7B What does justice mean to Christians?
• Write the Frequently Asked Questions (FAQ) page of a Buddhist website	• Renunciation • Enlightenment • Anicca • Anatta • Dukkha • Dhammapada • Eightfold Path • Dhammachakra	• Design a web page	✓7C Religious figure (generic) ✓✓7D Who was Gotama Buddha? ✓7D Who was Gotama Buddha?
• Design a leaflet for pupils to use when they visit a Buddhist centre	• Nirvana • Three Jewels • Sangha • Five Precepts • Meditation	• Word process leaflet • Scan pictures • Virtual tours of Buddhist temples	✓7C Religious figure (generic) ✓7D Who was Gotama Buddha?

✓✓close link

✓part link

Contents

Final task	Key words	ICT opportunities	QCA links
• Make a 'Wonder and Worry Wall' to show your hopes and fears about the environment • Write a personal action plan	• Sacred • Creation • Pollution • Stewardship • Interdependence	• Research environmental issues on websites • Word process the 'Wonder and Worry Wall'	✓✓7E What are we doing to the environment?
• Group presentation and personal response	• Moral dilemma • Vegetarian • Vivisection • Reincarnation • Krishna	• Powerpoint presentation of group's views	✓7E What are we doing to the environment?

✓✓close link
✓part link

What is RE?

● **What's the matter with Clucker?**

Clucker's moment for entry into the big wide world has arrived! But . . .

Outcome By the end of this unit you will understand what is important about RE.

Literacy Use key words, share ideas, draft and write captions and commentary, make notes, use glossary.

Final task Make a bookmark using word processing or DTP software.

Task 1

Tell Clucker's story.

1 Write a 'thought bubble' for each picture, with your ideas of what Clucker is feeling at each stage of the story. Think about: anxiety, excitement, uncertainty, curiosity, fear, wonder...

Now think about what you can learn from Clucker's story.

2 Think about any times when you felt like Clucker, perhaps when starting a new school, performing for the first time in front of an audience or meeting a new family member. Write some sentences to explain how you felt and why you felt like that.

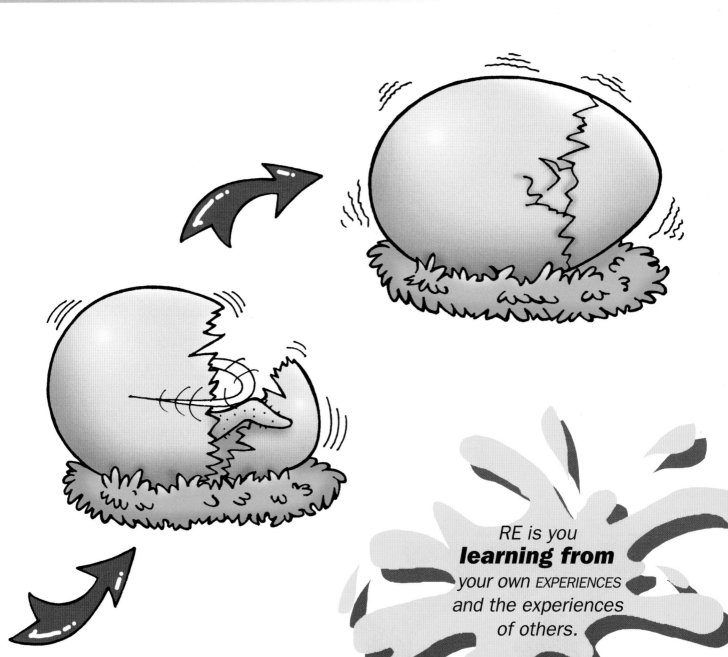

RE is you **learning from** your own EXPERIENCES and the experiences of others.

● Is there a God?

Look at Figure A. Write down these words and their meanings: THEIST, ATHEIST and AGNOSTIC.

A

B

Is God here? In the universe?

C

Is God here? In human love and happiness?

D

Is God here? In human suffering? Or in human help?

Is God here? In nature?

Task 3

When people explain why they do or do not believe in God, they often use an ARGUMENT (a thought-out reason) based on what they see happening in the world. For example they might say:

'There can't be a God because a God would stop natural disasters from happening.'

Or:

'There must be a God because if there was not, everyone would be selfish and just do what they wanted.'

a) Discuss Photographs B–E with a partner. They show some possible ways we might find God and reasons we might doubt God. Make a list of both.
b) Write down one argument that a theist might use to explain why they believe in God.
c) Write down one argument an atheist might use to explain why they don't believe in God.

E

*RE is **finding out why** some people believe in God and some do not.*

● What do you know about world religions?

Three-quarters of people in the world – and in Britain – have a religious BELIEF. Here are some words and symbols from the main world RELIGIONS they follow. These are also the six religions that you will study in this series.

Jesus

Bible

Qur'an

Shrine/temple

Siddattha Gotama

Vedas

Guru Granth Sahib

Church/chapel

Synagogue

Mosque

Torah

Task 4

RE is not new to you. You will have studied some of these religions before. See how well you can sort some information about the six religions. Copy this chart into your book and sort the words and symbols into the right boxes (one box willl be left blank). If you need extra help, try looking in RE books, in the library, using CD-ROMs or the internet, or asking!

Religion	Symbol	Founder or important leader	Sacred writing	Place of worship
Buddhism				
Christianity				
Hinduism				
Islam				
Judaism				
Sikhism				

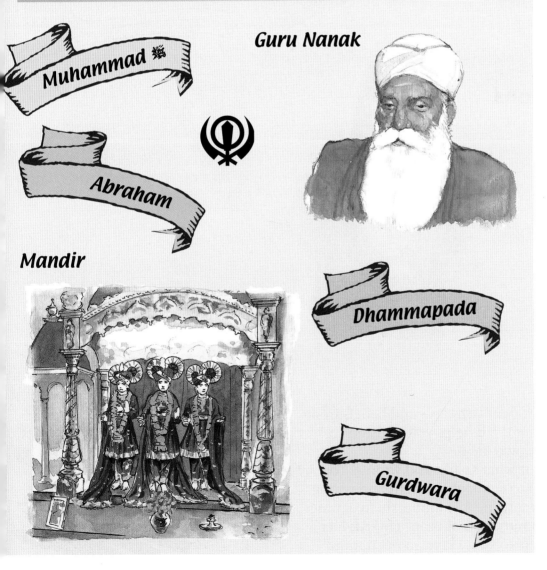

Muhammad

Guru Nanak

Abraham

Mandir

Dhammapada

Gurdwara

Hinduism
(*c.* 4000 years old)

Judaism
(4000 years old)

Buddhism
(2500 years old)

Christianity
(2000 years old)

Islam
(1400 years old)

Sikhism
(500 years old)

RE is **learning about** *world religions.*

Facts, opinions and beliefs...

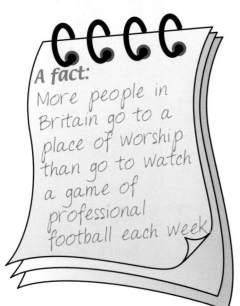

A fact:
More people in Britain go to a place of worship than go to watch a game of professional football each week

An opinion:
Religious buildings are a waste of money.

A belief:
I believe in life after death.

...and BIG questions

Is there a purpose to my life?

What is right and what is wrong?

- Do you feel you have different OPINIONS and beliefs from other people? Discuss them! RE helps you to listen to others and to share your own ideas.
- Do you feel puzzled about what's right and wrong? You are not alone! RE helps you to think about right and wrong.
- Do you wonder why so many people follow the teachings of religious leaders from hundreds of years ago? RE lets them explain their beliefs to you. Have an open mind!

RE includes some important facts but RE is also about **your** opinions, **your** beliefs and **your** questions.

So ... what is RE?

You are now going to make a bookmark to use in your notebook or put on display. The bookmark should have **RE** written at the top. Then add pictures, symbols and words to describe what RE and the different religions are all about. Look at this example and then design your own, using some of the ideas from the work you have done on pages 2–8.

2

How and why do people worship?

PRODUCTION COMPANY

Dear Researcher

Welcome to the research team for our TV feature programme about worship.

Our viewers are 9–13 year olds and the subject of our programme is religious worship. Worship means to show love and respect for God. It is an important part of any religion. We are going to focus on what religious believers do when they come together at a place of worship. Our aim is to help viewers to understand what's going on when people worship.

The programme will be called *Shoots and Roots*.

Let me explain:

A growing plant has shoots that are visible above the soil. This is what you can see.
But what you can't see is what is underneath the ground, the roots which keep the plant alive.

Our programme will describe worship in this way.

- There are things you **can** see happening – the things religious people say and do.
- There are things you **can't** see – hidden thoughts, feelings, beliefs and attitudes.

And remember, what you can't see is as important as what you can see.

To keep it simple we will concentrate on just one religion. We have chosen **Hinduism** – one of the oldest religions in the world. You may already know something about Hinduism. If not, then you are learning as you go, just like our viewers.

Good luck with your research!

Best wishes

Jo McDonald

PRODUCER OF CHILDREN'S PROGRAMMES

Religion   Hinduism as a case study.

Outcomes   By the end of this unit you will:

- understand what worship means
- understand how Hindus worship
- be able to explain how worship makes faith grow stronger.

Literacy   Use key words, research, select information, write a report.

Final task   Research and write a report on worship for a children's TV news programme.

Task 1

Read the letter carefully before you start your research. Make sure you are clear about what you have to do. Look at page 25 to see how you willl be asked to write your report.

1 Read how the letter explains **worship**. Write down a definition of worship in your own words.

2 On a large piece of paper, make your own drawing of a plant like this one. Draw a line across it to separate the top half – things you **can** see – from the bottom half – things you **can't** see.

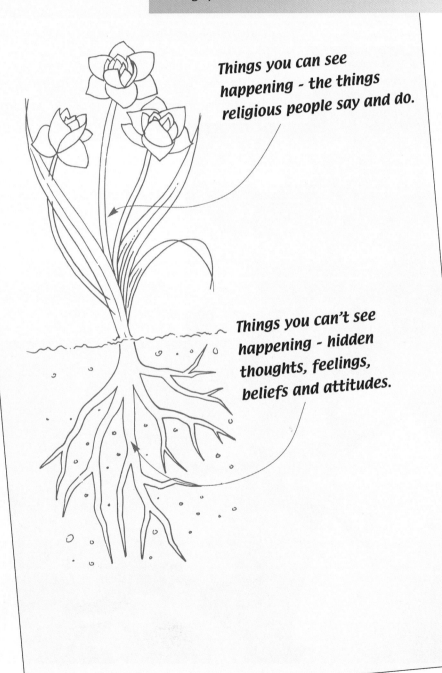

Things you can see happening - the things religious people say and do.

Things you can't see happening - hidden thoughts, feelings, beliefs and attitudes.

It would be very useful if you now went out to visit a Hindu place of worship in your own area. In case you can't, pages 12–23 will show you the most important aspects. Hinduism is a complex religion so these pages simplify things quite a lot. For example, the word 'God' is used in this unit for simplicity, but Hindus have many interpretations of what the word 'God' actually means, perhaps quite different from the meaning you are used to.

● **Welcome to the mandir**

Hindus can worship anywhere. Devout Hindus worship at home every day. Most Hindus also go to a temple or MANDIR. They pray, MEDITATE, eat, laugh and listen. One of the most attractive aspects of worshipping with other believers is just to enjoy meeting with friends. Meeting together makes people feel connected to other believers and part of a community. Music is also very important. Sometimes people just listen to the music but they also sing songs together.

Task 2

Work in pairs. One of you holds this book, the other closes their eyes.

1 **a)** Describe to your partner everything you can see in Photograph A.
   b) Swap roles and get your partner to describe Photograph B.
2 On your own, write some sentences describing one of these scenes of worship inside a mandir. For example: 'The people are holding lamps and candles.' 'They are looking at the shrine.' Try to convey the atmosphere.
3 Make a list of your own questions about Hindu worship. By the end of this unit you should be able to answer some of them.

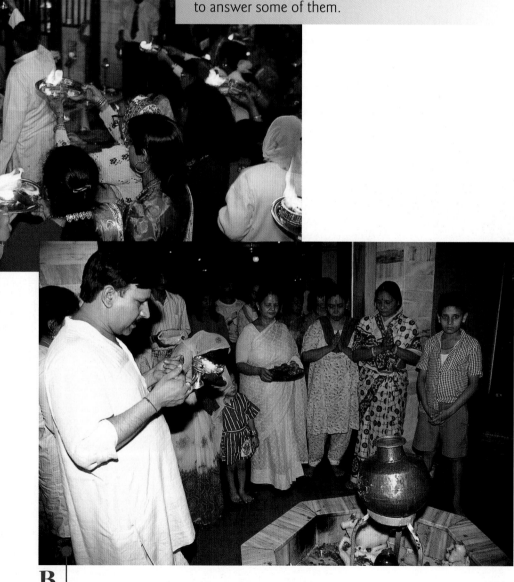

A

B

● **Is God in the shrine?**

It's obvious, as soon as you enter a mandir, that everyone's attention is
focused on the SHRINE. See if you can find out why.

C A Hindu shrine.

Task 3

Look carefully at Photograph C.

1 On your plant drawing from page 11, write notes in the **top half** about what you
can see in the shrine. Keep your diagram for the next task.
2 How do you know, just by looking, that the shrine is very important?

How do the murtis help Hindus to worship?

In the shrine there are images called MURTIS. The murtis look freshly washed and the clothes look new. Some religions forbid images of God because they think worshippers will worship the image rather than God. Hindus don't agree. They think images help people to worship and to feel close to God.

We offer to God the kinds of gift you would give to an honoured guest, such as flowers. But what is important is not the flowers themselves but the thinking behind them. In one of our holy books, God says:
> 'Whatever a keen soul may offer
> Be it a leaf, a flower, fruit or water,
> That I willingly accept
> For it was given in love.'

A Hindu worshipper reads from the Bhagavad Gita.

Murtis at the shrine. Krishna is on the left.

Task 4

The statements on pages 14–15 describe Hindu beliefs about God and explain why there are murtis in the shrine.

Sort the statements into two sets:

1 What Hindus believe about God.
2 Why Hindus have murtis, such as KRISHNA, in the shrine.

Focusing on the murti helps us to focus on BRAHMAN.

Other murtis represent different aspects of Brahman.

We believe in a supreme being that we call Brahman, whose spirit is everywhere.

Brahman is the spirit that is in everything.

Krishna is one of the most popular forms of Vishnu.

Krishna came to Earth to overcome evil and bring goodness and love.

Brahma, Vishnu and Shiva are the trimurti (three gods) who represent Brahman to the world.

We each choose our own murtis.

We can't imagine what Brahman is like – we're only human!

Individual Hindus may use more than one murti to help them worship.

When Hindus worship a murti of Krishna they remember all the things that Krishna did.

Brahma is the creator.
Vishnu looks after the creation.
Shiva destroys and recreates.
Vishnu came to Earth in many forms, one of which was Krishna.
Krishna is one of the most popular and respected gods in Hinduism.

Task 5

1 Look again at your plant drawing from page 11. In the **bottom half**, write notes about what Hindus believe about the murtis and how the murtis help them to worship. Keep your drawing. You will need it for your final task.
2 Read what the worshipper says on page 14. Write a sentence to explain why you think worshippers place flowers and pictures at the shrine.

● How do Hindus pray?

Prayer is a feature of nearly all religions. Prayer means talking to God.
Here are some examples of Hindu prayers.

1 From the unreal, lead me to the real!
From the darkness, lead me to the light!
From death, lead me to immortality.

2 O God! You are the giver of life,
The healer of pains and sorrows,
The giver of happiness.
O creator of the Universe,
Send us your purifying light
And lead our thoughts in your ways.

3 You my mother, you my father,
You my friend, you my teacher,
You my wisdom, you my riches,
You my all, O God of all gods.

D

E

Task 6

Read the prayers, then with a partner, discuss these questions:

1 Match each prayer to one picture. Give reasons for your choice.
2 **a)** Which prayer makes Brahman seem near and personal?
  b) Which prayer makes Brahman seem great and untouchable?
  c) One prayer says Brahman is 'the giver of life'. Find four other qualities of Brahman described in the prayers.
3 What does the speaker ask for at the end of the second prayer? Write in your own words.
4 On your own, choose one phrase from each prayer that you think could be used in worship by any religious person, not just a Hindu. Write a sentence to explain each choice.

F

What's going on below the surface when Hindus pray?

Hindus pray for different reasons. Sometimes they ask God for something, or thank God for something. Sometimes they pray because they are worried, or because they are happy. They often pray because they find it helps them to feel at peace with God. When they pray, they come into the presence of a power much bigger than themselves; a power that is in every part of the universe. They may pray at the start of the day, or at the end, or at any time.

There is no fixed way for Hindus to pray; no fixed words; no fixed postures; but the photographs on pages 18–19 show some typical ways of praying. How people pray can reflect what they are feeling inside.

H

G

I

J |

K |

Task 7

1 Look closely at each of the pictures. Look at the people's postures (the way they are standing, sitting or kneeling). Look at what they are doing with their hands.
2 Now look at this list of words and phrases. Which do you think might apply to each person praying? Some might match more than one picture; some feelings might not apply to any picture – you decide.

   humble   focused   peaceful   hopeful   sad   close to God   calm
   connected   happy   thankful   ready to receive   cared for   overwhelmed
   part of a community   ready to face the world   loved

3 Look again at your plant drawing. In the top half – things you can see – write notes about the **words and actions** used by Hindus when they pray.

   In the bottom half – things you can't see – write notes about how you think **they feel**. If necessary, make another copy of the drawing. Keep your notes. You will need them for your final task.

● What is a ritual?

Many religions use RITUALS. A ritual is an action used again and again in exactly the same way. Repetition doesn't make them boring. In fact, the opposite is true – it makes them stronger.

To illustrate this, pages 20–21 show some rituals that are nothing to do with religion. These are rituals associated with important football matches.

Before the match

The teams line up to sing their national anthems.

The captains shake hands with each other and exchange pennants.

During the match...

There are many different rituals when a goal is scored! Each striker has his own special routine.

At the end

When the cup is given, the winning captain turns round and raises it to the cheering crowd.

The team parades around the ground, carrying the trophy.

Team photographs are taken.

Task 8

1 Choose one football ritual that you think is particularly important. It could be one from pages 20–21, or another one you know about. Explain why you have chosen it.

2 With a partner, discuss and then note down two other examples of rituals in everyday life. For example: 'I always go to my gran's for tea on Fridays' or 'I always go swimming on my birthday'.

3 Work out two reasons why rituals in everyday life are important and why we seem to need them.

On pages 22–23, you will investigate a religious ritual.

● How does the Puja ritual help Hindus to worship?

The word 'PUJA' means worship. Items on the Puja tray help Hindus to show their love and devotion to God. The items also help Hindus to praise God for the elements: fire, water, air and earth. Hindus can use the Puja ritual together at the mandir or at home on their own or with their family.

A Puja tray.

Lamp burning butter

Bell

Water

Food

Flowers

Dish containing sandalwood paste

Incense stick

A family preparing for the Puja ritual.

Task 9

Statements **A–G** explain how Hindus use the items on the Puja tray.

1 Match each of the statements to one of the items.
2 In the middle of a large piece of paper, make your own simple line drawing of the Puja tray. Use the drawing on the left to help you.
   a) Down the left-hand side list the items on the tray (**what you can see**).
   b) Down the right-hand side write key words to remind you of what these things stand for or symbolise (**what you can't see**). Keep your drawing. You will need it for the final task.
3 Hindus use all their five senses in the Puja ritual. Write down one example in the Puja ritual for each of the senses: touch, smell, taste, hearing and sight.
4 Write a sentence to explain why you think using all five senses might help someone to worship better than if they used just one.

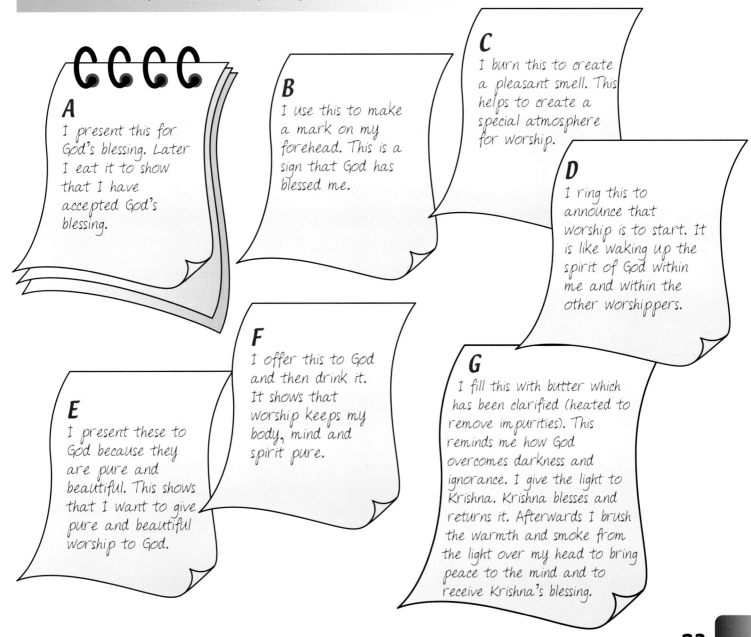

A
I present this for God's blessing. Later I eat it to show that I have accepted God's blessing.

B
I use this to make a mark on my forehead. This is a sign that God has blessed me.

C
I burn this to create a pleasant smell. This helps to create a special atmosphere for worship.

D
I ring this to announce that worship is to start. It is like waking up the spirit of God within me and within the other worshippers.

E
I present these to God because they are pure and beautiful. This shows that I want to give pure and beautiful worship to God.

F
I offer this to God and then drink it. It shows that worship keeps my body, mind and spirit pure.

G
I fill this with butter which has been clarified (heated to remove impurities). This reminds me how God overcomes darkness and ignorance. I give the light to Krishna. Krishna blesses and returns it. Afterwards I brush the warmth and smoke from the light over my head to bring peace to the mind and to receive Krishna's blessing.

Prepare for the final task

1 Gather together your work on this unit to prepare for the final task.

2 Write your answers to these questions in your book. You can find the answers on pages 10–23:

   a) What does the word **worship** mean?
   b) Do people have to go to a special building to worship?
   c) What is prayer?
   d) What is a ritual?

3 Re-read the instructions from the television producer in her letter on page 10:

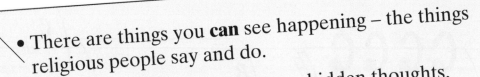

- There are things you **can** see happening – the things religious people say and do.

- There are things you **can't** see – hidden thoughts, feelings, beliefs and attitudes.

4 Check! You should have these notes:

   - a description of worship at the mandir from page 12
   - one or two plant diagrams about the shrine, the murtis and prayer, from pages 11–19
   - a line drawing of the Puja tray and your comments on it from page 23.

   You will use these notes and diagrams to help you to write your report to the producer of *Shoots and Roots*.

5 Look back over your diagrams. Highlight the most important ideas. On each diagram add one sentence to explain how this might help a Hindu believer to worship.

Final task

So ... how and why do people worship?

You are now ready to write your final report. It should have three main sections:

1 the shrine
2 prayer
3 the Puja ritual,
plus an introduction and a conclusion.

For sections 1–3 give your diagrams to the producer, then write a page of explanation picking out the key ideas.

SHOOTS

ROOTS

To: Jo McDonald
Producer, Children's Programmes, MM TV
From: (*your name here*)

WORSHIP RESEARCH PROJECT: FINAL REPORT

Introduction

Explain your task

1 The shrine
The first thing I investigated was a Hindu shrine. Anyone who visits a mandir would see . . .

Describe the shrine. How can you tell it is important?

Looking below the surface I tried to find out what the shrine told me about Hindu beliefs. The main things I found out were . . .

Beliefs about God – how murtis help

2 Prayer
I then studied Hindu prayer. What struck me most about how a Hindu prays was . . .

How do Hindus pray?

What is interesting is how people feel when they pray. This varies but I discovered that . . .

Give two examples

3 The Puja ritual
Finally, I looked at the Hindu Puja ritual. This is . . .

What happens in Puja? Give two examples

The Puja ritual helps the faith of the believer by . . .

How Puja helps

Conclusion

Summarise how worship makes faith grow stronger

What is the 'Big Story' told in the Bible?

● The big story?

Christians believe that the Bible tells one 'big story'. Some Christians believe that everything in the Bible is literally true, that it all really happened. Other Christians believe that some parts of the Bible are written as metaphors (symbols) to explain a person's relationship with God.

The main theme of the story – God's love for people – is always the same.

You could read the full story for yourself, but most Bibles are well over a thousand pages! So, the main events have been retold here in four different ways: a poem and art (pages 26–33), a short story strip (pages 34–35) and then in just four words (page 36)!

Part One: Paradise

The Garden of Eden: *Adam and Eve*, a linocut by African artist John Muafangeja.

Religion   Christianity.

Outcomes   By the end of this unit you will:

- understand the big story told in the Bible
- decide how relevant the big story is to today's world.

Literacy   Re-draft a story, use key words, explain beliefs, take notes, present information in a new way, summarise key ideas, write a glossary.

Final task   Design a poster to illustrate how the Christian story is relevant in the world today.

How does this picture show that life was good in the Garden of Eden?

In the beginning, before the Earth,
There was chaos and darkness,
God created order and light,
    All was well.

In the east, in Eden, God made a garden,
God made a man and a woman and placed them in the garden,
    All was well.

The man and the woman lived peacefully with each other,
With the animals and with the plants and, most importantly,
With God.
    All was well.

But…

One thing troubled the man and the woman,
They wanted to know God's secrets.
They wanted to know who God was and what God was like,
These secrets had been hidden by God to protect the man and the woman,
But they thought they knew better than God
And they ate from a forbidden tree.

Disaster.

Sin entered the world.
The man and woman could no longer live in the garden,
God banished them from their peaceful place out into a wilderness.
    All was not well.

Angels with swords of fire were placed at the gates of the garden,
There was no way back.

Task 1

Read the poem on pages 26–33 in less than ten minutes. Yes, you can do it! Now answer these questions without looking back at the pages. According to the poem:

1 How did everything go wrong in the beginning?
2 How were people helped to live more peacefully in the wilderness?
3 How did God give people a final chance?

Part Two: Good times and bad

The *Adoration of the Golden Calf* by Nicholas Poussin. According to the Bible, after God gave Moses the ten commandments, Moses came down the mountain to find that the people had made this idol and had started to worship it.

Choose three people in the painting. Look at their faces. What do you think they are feeling?

Time passed,

The family of the man and the woman grew large.
But all was not well.

Sin was everywhere.
There was envy, jealousy, suffering and, worst of all,
Death.

The people tried to find their way back to God,
They built a high building to try to reach God, but it collapsed.
They made their own new gods,
But these had no power – they brought no peace or happiness.

God saw their suffering and tried to reach them,
God gave the people some commandments to help them to live more
peacefully in the wilderness.

Do not kill,
Do not steal,
Do not worship other gods.

God sent prophets to tell the people how to live,
But often the people would not listen.
God sent messages of hope that one day all would be well again.

There were some good times,
But it was never as wonderful as it had been in the garden.

Part Three: God sent Jesus to a troubled world

Mother and child by Sister Victoria Choi of the Missionary Sisters of the Sacred Heart of Jesus, Korea.

Why do you think the baby is shown with his arms spread out?

Why has the artist shown many different hands reaching towards Jesus?

Then the moment came.

It was time to give the people in the wilderness
A final chance to make all things well,
To find the garden again.

God's son JESUS was sent by God to free the people from the wilderness
    to teach them,
      to heal them,
        to save them,
          to turn them away from sin,
            to turn them back to God.

Part Four: Death – and resurrection

The tree of life: Christ on the cross, carved by African artist Tidjani Agona.

Why do you think the carving is called *The tree of life*, even though it shows death?

Jesus helped many people,

He frightened others,
And he angered many powerful people who wanted to get rid of him.

They killed the son of God.
This was a bleak day,
Evil had beaten good.
It seemed that the people had thrown away their last chance.

But it was not God's way to hate and punish.
Three days later, the deepest scar of all, the scar of death, was healed,
God raised Jesus back to life.
Hope returned,
Like a small seed planted in the wilderness.

Part Five: The birth of the Christian church

The Reredos Tapestry, by John Piper, hangs in Chichester Cathedral. Three central panels show the Trinity (God as Father, Son and Holy Spirit). The four side panels represent the four Gospel writers.

1 Discuss the picture with a partner. Pick five words to describe it, for example, 'colourful', 'mysterious'.

2 How does the artist show the effects of God's spirit breathing on the disciples?

3 Which parts of the poem below can you link with the different symbols in the tapestry?

In Jerusalem,

Jesus' disciples were praying.

Like a rushing wind, the spirit of God breathed upon them,
It was like a fluttering dove,
It was like tongues of fire,
It was like water nourishing the small seed of hope inside them,
The seed sprouted.

Suddenly these ordinary people knew the truth about Jesus,
Jesus was the Son of God,
Jesus was alive – forever!

Jesus' death was all part of a bigger plan to save the people.
Jesus offered the way back to God,
God had not left the Earth to drift hopelessly in the chaos.

They told everyone who would listen,
On that first day three thousand people became Christians,
The Christian church was born!

● The big Christian story in two pages

Task 2

Look carefully at all the pictures in the story on page 34.

1 Match each of the statements **A–J** with one frame of the story.
2 Imagine someone much younger than you is reading this completed story strip. Write a short glossary to go with it: define any words that you think they will not understand. Use a dictionary to help you. You could also use the glossary at the back of this book.

You need to know

This big Christian story grew out of the Jewish story. You will find out more about Jewish teachings later in the course.

A People tried their own mistaken ways to find their way back to God.

B God came to Earth in human form as Jesus to teach the people how to live: the INCARNATION

C Before the CREATION of the world, there was chaos.

D Moses passed on God's guidance through the ten commandments.

E Jesus came back to life in the RESURRECTION.

F God created a perfect world. It was like a garden.

G God's spirit lives on, bringing hope to the world.

H Prophets promised that one day God would bring peace.

I Adam and Eve disobeyed God and drifted away from God. Sin entered the world.

J Jesus prayed for forgiveness as he was CRUCIFIED by his enemies but it was all part of a bigger plan to save the people.

● The big Christian story in four words

You should know the Christian story quite well by now. Here it is in just four words.

Chaos & Creation
Sin & Hope

Christians believe that:

Where there is **CHAOS** God will bring **CREATION**

Where there is **SIN** God will give **HOPE**

> **The big Christian idea**
> Without God there is chaos. Things turn bad.
> With God there is hope. Things turn good.

The hard questions for you in this task, and for Christians everywhere, are 'What has this got to do with today's world? Is it relevant? Is it really true?'

Most Christians would say it is. Every Sunday in churches throughout the world you can hear Christian preachers trying to explain how this story is relevant to the modern world. In fact, working out **how** it is relevant is what being a Christian is all about. In the next unit you will look at one aspect of this – how the Christian story makes Christians work for justice. Through the rest of the course you will come back to this story several times.

For now you are simply going to consider where you think our world fits into this big story.

Final task

Where is your world in this big story?

Stage 1
  a) Work in groups of four. Take one of these words each: chaos, creation, sin, hope.
  b) Write your word in the centre of a large piece of paper.
  c) Around your word, write examples of it in the world today. You should be able to think of plenty, but to get started look at the pictures on this page.

Stage 2
Now express your own thoughts and feelings about your word visually. You could:
  a) draw a picture
  b) design a symbol, and add a note to explain it
  c) write and illustrate a poem
  d) make a collage of cuttings or images.
Add these to your word poster.

Stage 3
Put together your posters of words and images to make a four part display. Then write four short paragraphs about your own response to your display: one paragraph for each poster.

In your view which of the four words best describes the world today? Do you feel you live in:
A chaotic world?
A creative world?
A sinful world?
A hopeful world?

Come back to your group of four and discuss your responses to find out if you agree.

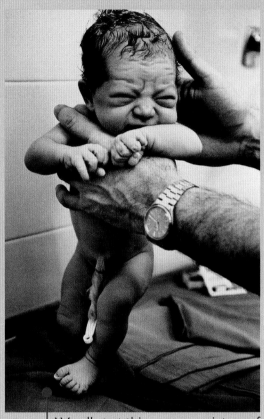

We all start this way – a mixture of genes that determine how we look and what we are like.

Children escape war-torn Liberia to play football in Britain and meet their footballing heroes.

Innocent people's homes and lives get destroyed by war.

4 What does justice mean to Christians?

Religion Christianity.

Outcomes By the end of this unit you will:

- know what Christians mean when they talk about justice
- understand why Christians believe Jesus wants them to work for justice
- see how some Christians work for justice
- respond in your own way to Jesus' vision of justice.

Literacy Read and analyse Bible extracts, role play, summarise, discuss, compose a poem, prayer or play.

Final task Design a poster with words and pictures to summarise Christian ideas about justice.

The Maria Cristina Gomez cross.

Maria's story

Maria Cristina Gomez was a teacher in El Salvador in Central America. She belonged to a church that tried to help poor people. She was an ordinary person but she lived in a country with big problems (you can read more about El Salvador on page 40).

Maria was a teacher in a town, but at weekends she went to nearby villages to help them. She taught people to read. She thought this was important because if you can't read, people can take advantage of you. If poor people learned to read and write then they could find out what was happening in El Salvador. They could stand up for their rights. They could become better farmers or be more healthy, because they could read leaflets telling them about more efficient farming methods or how to look after their children. Maria particularly worked with women.

In April 1989 armed men came to her school. In full view of her students they dragged her away and bundled her into a van. Friends later found her body dumped by a roadside. There were acid burns on her back and shoulders. Her face had been beaten and she had been shot four times. She had been murdered by air force officers working for the government of El Salvador.

The people who knew Maria wanted to remember her. So they paid an artist to paint the wooden cross which you can see on page 38. It shows the people who Maria helped and how she helped them.

Task 1

Discuss in groups:

1 Look carefully at the cross on page 38. What can you work out from this about Maria?
   a) Where is Maria?
   b) What is she doing?
   c) Note four other things this painting tells you about her.
2 Think about Maria's story. Why do you think the government wanted Maria killed?
3 At the centre of the cross Maria is shown with arms outstretched, just like pictures of Jesus on a cross. Why do you think the artist has done this?

● **What did justice mean to Maria Gomez?**

Maria Cristina Gomez believed in JUSTICE. Justice is an important part of Christianity. In this unit you will find out what it means to Christians. Let's start with what it meant to Maria.

Injustice in El Salvador

El Salvador is a small country in Central America.

For years it was ruled by its fourteen most powerful families. They were used to getting their own way. For example, if they wanted some land they moved the owners off it – without payment. They kept themselves rich and others poor.

This was unjust but it was hard to do anything about it. If you criticised the rulers or protested too much then soldiers might arrest you. You could be tortured or murdered. Ordinary people lived in fear.

Some people decided to start a war to get rid of the government. It lasted ten years. Around 70,000 people died.

Other people, like Maria Gomez, said that war was no way to bring justice to El Salvador. Instead they used peaceful methods to try to make the government act more fairly. But even these people were treated as troublemakers. Many were arrested and many were murdered. Oscar Romero – the leader of the Catholic church in El Salvador – was gunned down in front of his congregation because he criticised what the government was doing.

Pages 40–41 show you some of the things that Maria thought were unjust.

The rich were very rich and the poor had very little money.

The two sides in the civil war were fighting and many civilians were being caught in the crossfire. War was hurting everyone in El Salvador. Maria wanted the two sides in the civil war to reach a peaceful agreement.

Poor people were thrown off land that they had farmed for years.

Ordinary people got no education. They could not read so they could not stand up for their rights: if you can't read or write you can't even read the instructions on a bottle of medicine for your child.

Women were treated as second class citizens. The men expected them to stay in the background. They worked hard but were never CONSULTED about things that affected their lives.

Most people had no say in who ran El Salvador. They could not elect new leaders because the elections were not fairly run.

There were not enough doctors. And poor people could not afford to see a doctor.

DOCTOR 173 km

People were put in prison or even killed just because they criticised the government.

These situations of injustice are repeated in many countries around the world.

- **POVERTY**
  Money and resources are not shared fairly between people or between countries.
- **POWERLESSNESS**
  Some people use their power to harm others, not to help them.
- **RACISM**
  People of one race sometimes mistreat members of another race or religion.

Many Christians believe that God is not happy with this. They try to change it.

They believe that if the world was run by God's values:

- There would be fairer shares for everyone.
- There would be no racial discrimination.
- Everyone would have equal rights.
- People would use their power to help others, not to harm them.

Christians have a vision of **a fairer world**. This is what they mean by **justice**.

Maria Gomez believed that God wanted justice in El Salvador. Her friends believe that she died because she wanted justice in El Salvador. It was so important to her that she was prepared to risk her life.

Task 2

Look at the eight examples of injustice on pages 40–41. Work with a partner.

1 Discuss what you think is unjust about each situation.
2 Discuss what would need to change to make each situation more just.
3 **a)** On your own, take a large sheet of blank paper and copy this diagram:

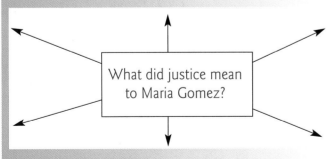

What did justice mean to Maria Gomez?

b) From your discussion of questions 1 and 2, add words, phrases or ideas about Maria and justice. Keep this diagram. You will need it for your final task.

Task 3

Write about your own vision of justice.

1 Write down ten ideas of how you would like to see a fairer world today.
2 With a partner, compare your visions. Keep them – you will need them on page 43.

● **What did justice mean to Jesus?**

Christians get their greatest inspiration from the life of Jesus. They try to think and to behave as Jesus would have done. Let's see what he had to say one day in his home town of Nazareth.

Jesus is at the synagogue. He has been asked to read to the crowd from the Jewish scriptures. The reading comes from the book of Isaiah. It is a famous passage that everyone in the synagogue knows very well. The story of Jesus reading this passage is reported in the book of Luke in the NEW TESTAMENT. Luke is one of the four gospels which give different accounts of what Jesus did and said.

The spirit of the Lord is upon me because he has chosen me to bring good news to the poor. He has sent me to proclaim liberty to the captives and recovery of sight to the blind, to set free the oppressed and announce that the time has come when the Lord will save his people.

Jesus says, 'This passage of scripture has come true today...'

The reaction of his listeners is first disbelief, then anger. This scripture, which everyone knows so well...Jesus is saying it is actually about him!

Jesus is just the village carpenter!

They turn on him.

They chase him out of the town.

They reject him.

But at this moment Jesus had set out his vision of justice for the world.

Task 4

1 Look at what Jesus says on page 42. Make a list of three groups of people Jesus says he wants to help. Look up words that you don't know in the dictionary.

2 What do you think Jesus meant by 'the Lord will save his people'? You might need to read the 'You need to know' box on page 45.

3 Why do you think the people chased Jesus out of town?

4 a) Take a large sheet of blank paper and copy this diagram:

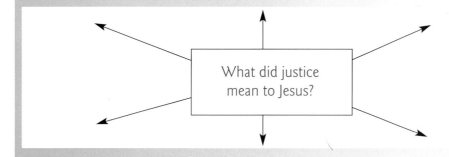

What did justice mean to Jesus?

b) From your answers to questions 1, 2 and 3, add words, phrases or ideas that Jesus would associate with justice.

Upside-down values

The people in Nazareth may have rejected Jesus but others were much more interested in what he had to say. It was often surprising. For example, at that time people thought that someone who was rich and powerful must be especially close to God. Surely God must have made them rich and powerful because God liked them! Jesus said no: God loves the weak, the poor and the oppressed.

Task 5

1 With a partner, discuss what you think about Jesus' vision of justice. How does it compare with your ideas from page 41?

2 Why do you think Jesus' ideas would appeal to people like Maria Gomez (pages 39–41)?

● How did Jesus show justice in his actions?

Jesus did more than just talk about justice. Here is an example of Jesus putting his words into action.

> *Jesus went on into Jericho and was passing through. There was a chief tax collector there named Zacchaeus, who was rich. He was trying to see who Jesus was, but he was a little man and could not see Jesus because of the crowd. So he ran ahead of the crowd and climbed a sycamore tree to see Jesus, who was going to pass that way. When Jesus came to that place, he looked up and said to Zacchaeus, 'Hurry down, Zacchaeus, because I must stay in your house today.'*
>
> *Zacchaeus hurried down and welcomed him with great joy. All the people who saw it started grumbling. 'This man has gone as a guest to the home of a sinner!'*
>
> *Zacchaeus stood up and said to the Lord, 'Listen, sir! I will give half my belongings to the poor, and if I cheated anyone, I will pay him back four times as much.'*
>
> *Jesus said to him, 'Salvation has come to this house today . . . the Son of Man came to seek and to save the lost.'*
>
> *Luke 19.1–10.*

What you have read on pages 38–44 makes Christians say that Jesus was 'on the side of' the poor and the powerless. His 'good news for the poor' was not just words – he actually wanted to change their situation, to turn unjust situations into just ones.

I'm a rich man but I'm an outcast. People hate me.

Zacchaeus is a sinner. He works for the Romans who are the enemies of God's people. Jews should have nothing to do with him.

Zacchaeus is a cheat. He overcharges us, but what can we do? He's got powerful friends.

Task 6

Understand the story

1 What was unjust about the situation before Jesus came along?
2 What did Jesus do to change it?
3 How did Jesus make the situation more just?

Turn your story into a radio news report

4 In groups of four, prepare a two-minute news feature for Radio Jericho. The headline should be **'Justice comes to Jericho!'** Any story about justice for the people in this Roman-occupied country is sure to be a winner – it could even make national headlines!

Your report should include:

a) interviews in which someone explains what Zacchaeus was like before Jesus came along. The drawings on page 44 will give you ideas.
b) an eyewitness account of what happened when Jesus came to Jericho.
c) some more interviews with the people from **a)** who say how the situation has changed for them now.

You can write your script or record it.

5 Rehearse and present your two-minute broadcast.

You need to know

Jesus lived in Palestine. At that time Palestine was controlled by rulers from the Roman Empire. They were sometimes very cruel. The Jews were forced to pay them taxes. A lot of Jewish people were hoping that a Messiah would come and get rid of the hated Romans for good.

● What did justice mean to Desmond Tutu?

In the 1950s Desmond Mpilo Tutu was a teacher in Krugersdorp. As a black teacher teaching black children he was ordered to teach only the most basic skills.

Some black leaders thought the only way to bring justice to South Africa was by armed struggle against the government. But not Desmond Tutu.

It was a very long struggle. Eventually the white government of South Africa gave in to the pressure.

You need to know

For many years, the people of South Africa lived under a system called APARTHEID. This was an unjust system of government. Black people were separated from white people: on buses, in schools, at the beach, at cinemas, at sports grounds. Black people had to live where they were told – on the poorest and most overcrowded land – well away from white areas. Black people had little freedom and lived in great poverty. They could not vote.

The Commission did not hold trials or punish anyone. Instead, both black and white South Africans told the truth about what they had done and sought the forgiveness of their victims.

46

3 "Apartheid will collapse one day because injustice is against the will of God. Justice will come to South Africa. We must believe that."

Tutu took a different path. He became a priest in the Anglican church, then later head of the South African Council of Churches.

4 "You cannot resist a violent regime by being violent yourself. We must work peacefully to bring justice to South Africa."

Tutu believed in justice. But he also believed in non-violence.

5

He helped to persuade other countries to stop buying South African goods until the government ended apartheid. To prevent him preaching this message the government took away his passport so that he could not travel abroad.

7

All the apartheid laws were scrapped. Black people could now vote. In April 1994, for the first time in his life, Tutu was allowed to vote.

8 "There is no future for South Africa without forgiveness. Revenge will lead to a bloodbath. Forgiving and forgetting will allow South Africa to move forward."

TRUTH AND RECONC

The new President, Nelson Mandela, gave Tutu a very important job. He put him in charge of South Africa's Truth and RECONCILIATION Commission. This investigated the crimes committed by all sides during the apartheid regime.

10 "Now you are in power do not forget the poor. They still need justice. Do not feather your own nest while you leave the schools, the houses and the hospitals in tatters."

Apartheid laws were ended but justice did not immediately come to South Africa. It takes a long time to undo years of injustice.

Task 7

I Make a third justice diagram like this:

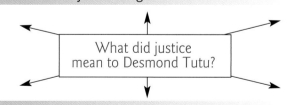

What did justice mean to Desmond Tutu?

2 Add words, phrases or ideas that Desmond Tutu would associate with justice. Keep this diagram. You will need it for your final task.

3 Discuss: do you think forgiving somebody is a strong or a weak thing to do? Give reasons.

4 Discuss: why might the story of Desmond Tutu's struggle against apartheid have appealed to Maria Gomez (page 39)?

● What did justice mean to the 'Good' Samaritan?

The parable of the Good Samaritan

Narrator	A religious teacher came to talk to Jesus.
Religious teacher	*What must I do to receive eternal life?*
Jesus	*What do the scriptures say?*
Religious teacher	*Love God with all your heart.*
Jesus	*and … ?*
Religious teacher	*…and love your NEIGHBOUR as yourself.*
Jesus	*You are right. Do this and you will live.*
Narrator	But the teacher wanted to show how clever he was.
Religious teacher	*(smugly) But tell me … who is my neighbour?*
Narrator	So Jesus told this story …

1

… There was a man, a Jew, travelling by himself on the steep and dangerous road from Jerusalem to Jericho.

2

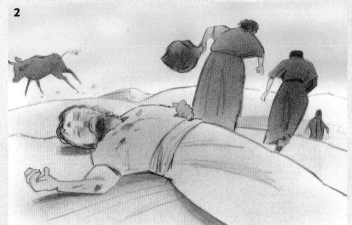

Suddenly, robbers leapt out and attacked him. They stole all his possessions, beat him savagely and left him for dead.

3

Later that day, a priest was walking along the road and saw the man lying there, but he did not want to get involved and he did not help him.

4

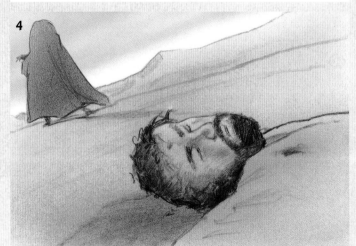

Later still, a LEVITE passed by, but he crossed the road, not wanting to have anything to do with the dying man.

5

Finally, a SAMARITAN came along. Brushing aside the normal prejudices, he helped the man and saved his life.

6

The Samaritan took the man to the nearest town and paid someone to take care of him until he was well enough to continue his journey ...

Narrator	When Jesus had finished his story, for a moment there was silence while everyone thought about the story, then...
Jesus	*Which of these three do you think acted as neighbour towards the man attacked by the robbers?*
Religious teacher	*The one who was kind to him.*
Jesus	*You go, then, and do the same.*

You need to know

- This story has become so familiar today that some readers miss how shocking it was. At the time of Jesus, Jews and Samaritans hated each other. So, for a Jew, there was no such thing as a 'good Samaritan'! Jesus said differently. This Samaritan was not put off by racial barriers. He did not say, 'I'll leave that man – he is a Jew,' but said, 'He needs help, so I'll help him.'
- The priest and the Levite were religious people. They might have been thinking fine thoughts, but they were not doing the right actions. They did not act justly. The Samaritan did.

Task 8

1 Which of the following is the best summary of the message of this PARABLE?
  a) Never trust a Samaritan.
  b) Help those who are suffering even if it means risking your own life.
  c) God judges a person by what they do for others, not by where they come from.
  d) Always look on the bright side of life.
2 What was unjust about the situation before the Good Samaritan came along?
3 How did the Good Samaritan's actions change things? Don't just think about the obvious things. Kind actions can eventually affect people who had nothing to do with the original situation.

● How can we help to bring justice to our world?

We are not all like Maria Gomez or Desmond Tutu. We live different lives in different countries with different problems. But whoever we are, we all have the power to help others. Jesus told a famous parable which made a similar point: justice can begin with small acts of kindness.

The parable of the sheep and the goats

When the Son of Man comes as king . . . The people of all nations will be gathered before him. Then he will divide them into two groups, just like a shepherd separates the sheep from the goats. He will put the righteous people on his right and the others on his left.

Then the king will say to the people on his right, 'Come and possess the kingdom that has been prepared for you ever since the creation of the world.

I was hungry and you fed me, thirsty and you gave me a drink;

I was a stranger and you received me into your homes, naked and you clothed me;

I was sick and you took care of me, in prison and you visited me.'

The righteous will then answer him, 'When, Lord, did we ever see you hungry and feed you, or thirsty and give you a drink?

When did we ever see you a stranger and welcome you into our homes, or naked and clothe you?

When did we ever see you sick or in prison, and visit you?'

The king will reply, 'I tell you, whenever you did this for one of the least important of these brothers of mine, you did it for me!'

From *Matthew* 25.31–40. You can look up what happened to 'the others on his left' in verses 41–46!

Task 9

1 With a partner, answer these questions:
   a) What was the reward for the righteous?
   b) What had the righteous done?
   c) Why were the righteous puzzled?
   d) What was the explanation for their reward?
2 Which of the following is the best explanation of the message of this parable?
   a) Make sure you don't become homeless, ill or a prisoner.
   b) Jesus was always in trouble.
   c) By helping people in need you are helping Jesus.
   d) Give money to charity.

A On the streets with nowhere to stay.

B Twenty-year sentence with nothing to look forward to.

C Alone and abandoned – the victim of a dictator's policy.

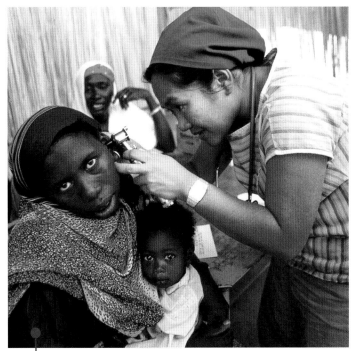

D Not enough doctors because all the money's gone to pay the country's debts.

Task 10

Look at Photographs A–D. How could people act with kindness in these situations? To show this, you could draw a picture, write a poem or a song, prepare a group dance or a freeze frame ... Think about what someone could do on their own to help, but also think about what they could do together with other people to change the situation for good. Give your work a title. It could be used in your final task, so if it is a dance or freeze frame, arrange for a photograph!

● So, what does justice mean to Christians?

Justice means standing up for powerless people and giving them a voice.

Anyone who:

- helps the poor or helps the poor to help themselves
- challenges powerful or selfish people to use their power to help others
- brings peace or reconciliation
- cares about others
- helps those in need
- is honest and unselfish

is continuing this work begun by Jesus.

For your final task, you need to show that you have understood Jesus' vision, and show what you think about it.

Look back through this unit.

Justice means:

- helping poor people, and speaking out against their oppressors.

- caring about others, whatever their race, colour or religion.

- helping the hungry, the homeless, the refugee...

- being a peacemaker and showing forgiveness.
- standing up for goodness, even when it's difficult.

- acting unselfishly, being honest, not cheating, and sharing wealth fairly.

Task 11

Look back to your three justice diagrams. They should include words and ideas that you think Christians associate with the word justice.

Think about which ideas are most important.

1 **a)** Write each idea on a separate piece of paper or card.
   b) Work with a partner or in a group. For each of the following people choose the meaning of the word 'justice' that would be the most important to them:
   - Maria Gomez
   - Jesus
   - Desmond Tutu.
   c) Write a sentence to explain your choice.

2 Now sort your cards into two piles: 'doing this would be **safe, causing no problems**' and 'doing this **could be risky**'
Discuss with your partner or group why the **risky** pile could be trouble for you and why the **safe** pile would not be troublesome.

3 'Religion is about God, not everyday life.' Write down your opinion of this statement.

Final task

So ... what does justice mean to Christians?
Design a poster based on what you have done in this unit. Your poster should show what you think justice means to Christians. It should include at least five different examples of how people still try to follow this vision in their daily lives.

This is the time when you choose the best of your ideas and present them. You can choose to include all pictures, or all words, or a mixture of both.

Include a short commentary explaining why you have selected these ideas.

5 Why was Gotama Buddha so special?

● **From wealthy prince to holy man. Why did he suddenly change?**

This image of the BUDDHA shows him in meditation. He was a troubled young Indian prince before he became the Buddha. He made a choice that changed his life forever.

Religion Buddhism.

Outcomes By the end of this unit you will:

- know about Gotama Buddha and the important choices he made about his life
- understand some of his teachings
- form your own opinion on the choices he made.

Literacy Interpret Buddhist stories and texts, discuss your opinions and thoughts, summarise information, write for a website.

Final task Write the Frequently Asked Questions (FAQ) page of a Buddhist website.

Task 1

What clues are there in this image about the character of the Buddha? Look at his gesture, posture and expression.

How did they know that the Buddha was so special?

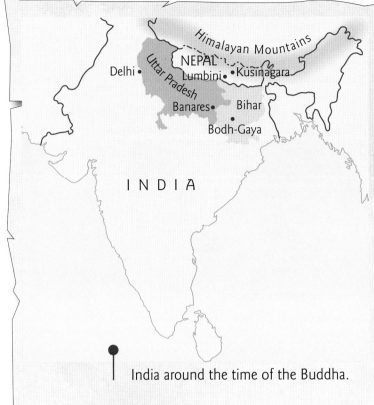

India around the time of the Buddha.

Two and a half thousand years ago, in the north-east of India, near the Himalayan mountains, a son was born to the king and queen of that kingdom. Before her pregnancy, Queen Maya had had a strange dream. She dreamt that a pure white elephant entered her side. Believing in the importance of dreams, she and the king went to ask their wisest advisers what it meant. The advisers told them that they would have a son who would be as rare and wonderful as the creature in Maya's dream.

As the time for the birth of her child drew near, Maya began the journey back to her parents' home but, on the way, Siddattha Gotama was born amongst a grove of trees at a place called Lumbini. To show how special he was, tradition says that at birth he was able to take seven steps and that he already had the marks of a great man, including the long tongue of a preacher.

Wise men told his parents that he had a great future ahead of him. But that future might be as a powerful ruler or as a holy man who gave up everything in the search for great truths. This troubled them for they were KSHATRIYA. It was their duty – and their son's – to be kings and warriors.

Maya never lived to see which choice her son made. She died when Siddattha was very young. But his father remembered the words of the wise men and kept watch over his son as he grew up. He had no intention of letting his son turn his back on power and wealth.

Task 2

1 Start collecting some information to help with your final task. Make a note of your answers to the following questions:
   a) Where and when was Siddattha Gotama born?
   b) Into what family was he born?
   c) What clues are in the text to suggest that he might have to make a difficult choice in the future?
2 Imagine you are Maya. You cannot forget the dreams or the words of the holy men. Write a letter to your son for him to read when he grows up, telling him about the choice he will have to make.

● The Buddha's early life

Although these two stories took place when Siddattha was young and still a prince, they give us a good insight into his ideas and feelings.

First story

He was taken by his father to watch the farmers harvesting their crops. As he watched, he fell into a sort of trance, thinking about the way nature moves in a cycle.

In this cycle, there is life as the crops grow, death as they are harvested and new life as the new seed is sown. The cycle is then repeated over and over again.

His thoughts did not trouble him. He felt calm and content as if he had understood something really important, not only about crops in the field but also about life.

Task 3

1 **a)** What does the second story tell you about Siddattha's character? For example, what do you think he felt about hunting? Write down words or sentences from the story which illustrate his feelings.
   b) Look up the word 'compassion' in the dictionary and write down what you find. How did Siddattha show compassion?
2 What do you think Siddattha learned in the two stories?

Second story

One day, whilst out in the forest with his cousin, Devadatta, Siddattha found a swan that had been wounded by an arrow fired from his cousin's bow. The sight of the injured creature upset him. He removed the arrow and took the bird back to the palace to care for it.

His cousin claimed angrily, 'The bird is mine! I shot it.' Siddattha could not part with it. 'Set the swan free,' he pleaded. 'No one can own it.'

Eventually they went to the wise men at the palace to ask them to decide who was the rightful owner. The wise men stated that the owner should be the person who had given the creature life, not the person who had tried to destroy it.

After he had nursed the bird back to life, Siddattha let it fly free.

Why did Siddattha's father try to tell him what to do?

As Siddattha grew older, the king sensed that his son was becoming restless. He tried his best to keep him amused, to stop him thinking about life. He wanted him to remain inside the palace, having a good time – fine foods, dancing, sport – the lot! That would mean all thoughts of becoming a holy man (a teacher of great truths) would never even enter his head!

The king even ordered that dead flowers should be removed before his son could see them. If any of his servants were ill, they had to stay in their rooms!

The king was trying to protect his son from the knowledge of what life is really like. He knew that if his son saw how rough life can be, he might start asking difficult questions and searching for great truths, just as the wise men had warned he would.

But all these fun times, all this protection, had the opposite effect. Instead of feeling happy, Siddattha felt stifled and bored with life.

Task 4

Discuss the following questions in groups.

1 Having a 'good time' is what life is all about.
   a) What do you think about that statement?
   b) Note down the main points for and against that view.
2 Which of your main points would Siddattha's father have chosen to defend his actions?

● **What happened to change Siddattha's life?**

Siddattha felt that something was missing from his life. And yet . . . by now, he had everything he could want, didn't he? Wealth, power, a beautiful wife and a baby son. But he felt a prisoner within the palace and one day persuaded his charioteer, Channa, to take him out into the city.

Prince Gotama leaves the palace.

The artist has shown four scenes happening in the same picture. The four scenes were turning points in Siddattha's life. They could be called life-changing experiences.

● Life-changing experiences for Siddattha

Siddattha is shocked by what he sees

Suddenly, Channa stopped the chariot. An old man was hobbling across the road. Siddattha burst out laughing. 'Why does he move like that? Is he dancing? And who painted his hair white and drew those lines on his face?'

Channa bit his lip. 'He's just old.'

'Old?'

'Everyone gets old. Our skin wrinkles and our hair turns white. We become weak and slow.'

Siddattha was shocked. 'Everyone?' he asked. 'But why? Why do we have to get old?' Channa shook his head. He didn't know.

A little further along, they came across a man moaning in pain.

'He doesn't sing very well,' Siddattha sighed.

'He's crying with pain,' Channa explained. 'He's sick.'

'Sick?'

'His body isn't working properly. It hurts him. Everyone's body can get sick and feel pain.'

Siddattha was horrified. 'Everyone's?' he asked. 'Even my father's? My wife's? Why? Why must we feel pain?' But Channa didn't know that, either.

The biggest shock of all came when they passed a funeral. The people carrying the body were weeping loudly.

'How can he sleep?' Siddattha was very puzzled. 'All that noise . . . ?' Channa hung his head.

'He is dead, my prince, not asleep. His life is gone.'

'Dead?' The prince looked and looked, unable to believe his eyes. 'Gone?'

'Everyone dies in the end. Every living thing.'

'Everyone?' Siddattha could feel tears stinging his eyes. 'But why?' he whispered. Then he too hung his head. 'Take me back, Channa,' he begged.

From *The Life of the Buddha* by Sally Humble-Jackson.

Task 5

Siddattha was beginning to understand how difficult and uncertain life can be.

I Imagine you are Siddattha. You have just returned from your chariot ride. You meet your father. Write a short conversation beginning:

> *Father: What's happened? You look dreadful!*
>
> *Siddattha: Why did you keep the truth from me?*

2 Siddattha found it difficult to accept what life is like – we are born, we grow up, we grow old, we die. With a partner, discuss what you feel about this and then write down your own thoughts. This will form an important part of your final task.

● **What was Siddattha's decision?**

The fourth scene in the painting on page 58 shows a robed holy man.

When Siddattha saw him, looking calm and peaceful, he questioned Channa for the fourth time.

'He is a holy man,' Channa explained. 'He has left family and possessions behind so that he can search for the truth about being happy in life.'

Siddattha thought of all that he had seen on his chariot ride. He felt very sad. How could people be happy in life, when there was so much sorrow and suffering?

He had to go in search of the answer. This would be a great turning point in his life. It was really hard to face up to, but he knew he must do it. It was a time of RENUNCIATION, giving up his old life at the palace. He was twenty-nine years old. The words of the wise men at his birth were coming true!

● **Siddattha searches for the answer**

How can people be happy in life when there is so much sorrow and suffering?

For six years Siddattha went from one teacher to another. He followed all sorts of advice. Nothing helped him to find the answer. Finally, he lived as a holy man, totally neglecting his body. Perhaps, he thought, in this way his mind would grow stronger. But he nearly died. He had moved from one extreme to the other, from giving the body everything to giving the body nothing. Neither way helped him to find the answer.

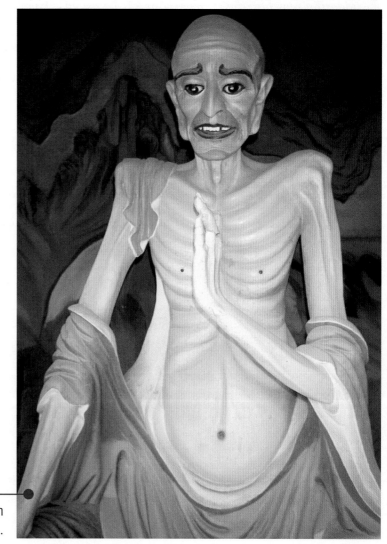

Starving Buddha. The Buddha ignored his body in order to develop his mind.

Task 6

1 List or draw four reasons why Siddattha's decision to leave was so difficult.

2 Leaving the palace was like coming to a crossroads in his life. He decided to do what he thought was the right thing. This can be difficult for anyone. Describe a situation when you had to make a choice between right and wrong.

Finally Siddattha remembered a story he had heard a musician tell about the sitar.

If you make the string too tight, it will snap. If you leave it too slack, it will not play. Either way – no tune. The middle way between these two extremes means you can play the tune.

Siddattha realised that he was like the strings of the sitar. He needed to follow a middle way between the two extremes.

● How did Siddattha find the answer?

He knew that he had to calm and clear his mind if he was going to discover the answer to his question. He remembered the trance he had fallen into as a boy watching the harvest. He sat under a Bodhi (fig) tree, determined to stay there until he found the truth. Bodhi means wisdom and the Bodhi tree is sometimes called the tree of wisdom. He went into a deep meditation that lasted all night. It was 528 BCE.

During the night, his mind struggled with many difficult temptations sent by Mara (the force of evil): temptations to give up his search, to give in to his desires for life's luxuries and pleasures, to let himself get angry and jealous. He resisted the temptations, placing his right hand on the ground as a way of showing that the Earth had witnessed his struggle.

As morning dawned, Siddattha felt that, at last, he really understood what caused people's sadness and suffering. For him, it was like waking up to the truth! From this time on, he became known as the Buddha, which means 'The Enlightened One' and his experience is known as the ENLIGHTENMENT.

Task 7

Meditation helped Siddattha to keep a calm and clear mind. Many people who are not Buddhists use some form of meditation to help them be calm. A very simple method involves concentrating on your breathing.

When you dwell on the sound of your breathing, when you can really hear it coming and going, peace will not be far behind...

Work out your own meditation exercise to keep calm.

What were Siddattha's three main thoughts?

1 Nothing ever stays the same. Everything and everyone in the world is always changing. Buddhists call this ANICCA.

2 If everything and everyone is always changing, then there can be no such thing as a permanent self. Buddhists call this ANATTA.

3 We want to be certain and safe and we try to find things and people that will make us feel that way. But this never works because we change – we grow old, get sick and die – and so do other people. Things wear out, get spoilt or go out of date. All this makes us feel uncertain and sometimes sad. Buddhists call this DUKKHA.

Buddhists call these the 'three marks of life'.

If everything is always changing, it can't stay the same. This means that you can change for the better – or the worse! You are in control.
　　You want to be good at sport? You need to practise.
　　You hope to do well at school? You need to work hard.

How are you always changing?

Task 8

The cells in your body are always changing, so are you the same person you were? You do not have the same ideas, beliefs and interests you had even five years ago. (Remember Father Christmas and the tooth fairy?) Try to think of something that does **not** change.

1 Look at the picture above. Is 60-year-old John the same person as 10-month-old John?
2 Present a poster or poem to express the Buddhist belief that you are always changing. You are not the same person you used to be! You could call it, *The Real Me?* or *Who am I?* or make up your own title. You could use this in your final task.
3 Think of all the ways in which you have changed, not just physically. Change can be both exciting and scary. How does it make you feel? Try to include your thoughts and feelings about change in your poster or poem.

● **What did the Buddha teach about suffering?**

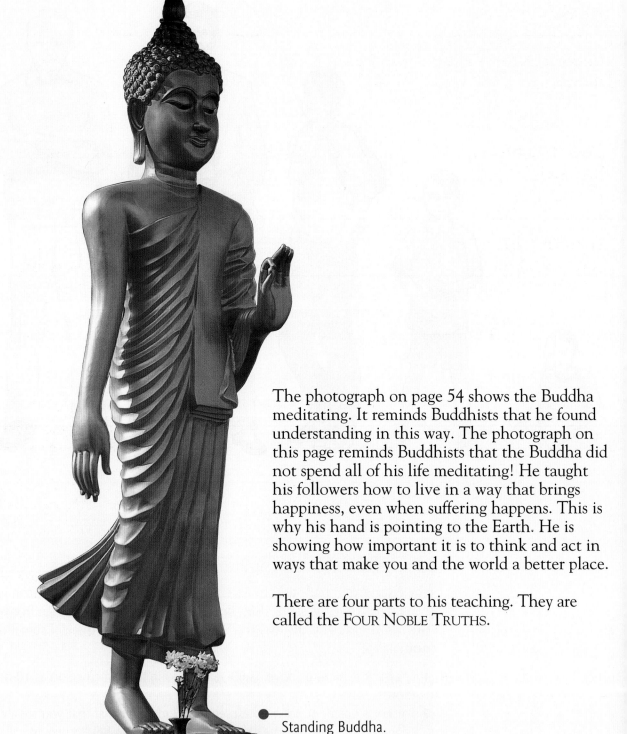

The photograph on page 54 shows the Buddha meditating. It reminds Buddhists that he found understanding in this way. The photograph on this page reminds Buddhists that the Buddha did not spend all of his life meditating! He taught his followers how to live in a way that brings happiness, even when suffering happens. This is why his hand is pointing to the Earth. He is showing how important it is to think and act in ways that make you and the world a better place.

There are four parts to his teaching. They are called the FOUR NOBLE TRUTHS.

Standing Buddha.

The Four Noble Truths

First Noble Truth: the facts	There will always be some form of suffering in life or a feeling that life is not perfect.
Second Noble Truth: the reason?	Suffering is caused by wanting more and more things. This feeling of wanting cannot bring happiness because things are always changing .
Third Noble Truth: the answer?	Accept that things change. Treasure each moment, living the best way you can. Don't be self-centred. If you live in a way that is good and helps others, you will be happy.
Fourth Noble Truth: how to go about it?	Follow the advice given in the Noble EIGHTFOLD PATH. This Path sets out the Buddha's guidance on the way to live so that you are at peace with yourself and the world. The details are on pages 68–69.

Task 9

1 Write down three things that you really want in life and why you want them. You might be desperate for the latest designer trainers or something very different, such as a healthy body.
2 Work with a partner. Explain why you want the things on your list. Your partner thinks of reasons why getting the things on your list won't give you lasting happiness. For example, 'you'll soon grow out of the trainers', or 'having a healthy body isn't the only thing to make you a happy person'.
3 Now do the same for the things on your partner's list.
4 Write three sentences to explain how your lists could be an example of the Second Noble Truth.

● Why was Gotama Buddha so special?

The Buddha travelled around India for over forty years and the numbers of his followers grew. Among them were members of his own family. All his followers were helped by his calm manner and wise teaching. They understood his teaching and it helped them to know how to live. He died when he was eighty.

The Buddha was not a god. He was a human being. But his teachings – known as the DHAMMA – are still followed today by millions of people all over the world.

Here is what some Buddhists say:

Words of wisdom

The DHAMMAPADA is a book containing the words of the Buddha. Here are the opening words:

> If one speaks or acts with a wicked mind, unhappiness follows even as the wheel follows the hoof of an ox.
>
> Similarly, if one speaks or acts with a pure mind, happiness follows like a shadow that never ceases.

In other words, **actions have consequences**:

- The more you think and do good things, the better you will become.
- The more you think and do bad things, the worse you will become.

Nothing happens by chance, but by the law of cause and effect. Actions from earlier in your life bring you to certain situations.

It is your own actions that bring you happiness or suffering. You have to take responsibility for yourself.

There is no point in acting immorally because you will only suffer yourself in the end.

Task 10

This may help with section 3 of your final task.

1 In pairs, work out a short story to show the idea that actions have consequences. It should tell of a situation where a **bad** deed leads to a **bad** outcome. You could present your story in written form, or as four or five simple line drawings, which must:
   a) set the scene and introduce the characters
   b) show what happened and the choice made
   c) make the outcome clear.

2 Exchange your story with another pair of pupils. Use their story but this time show how a **good** deed might have changed the outcome.

3 Discuss the differences between the outcomes.

Final task

So ... why was Gotama Buddha so special?

Design a Frequently Asked Questions (FAQ) page for a website about Buddhism, in three sections:

1 Siddattha Gotama: prince turned holy man
2 The Buddha's teachings
3 Buddhism today: why learn about Gotama Buddha?

Use your notes from this unit to create a web page that could be used by other pupils. Answer the questions from the sample page below, and write some of your own.

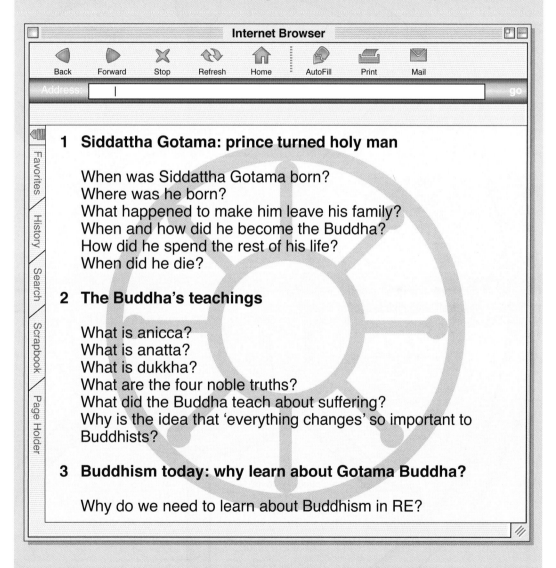

Internet Browser

Back   Forward   Stop   Refresh   Home   AutoFill   Print   Mail

Address: go

Favorites | History | Search | Scrapbook | Page Holder

1   Siddattha Gotama: prince turned holy man

When was Siddattha Gotama born?
Where was he born?
What happened to make him leave his family?
When and how did he become the Buddha?
How did he spend the rest of his life?
When did he die?

2   The Buddha's teachings

What is anicca?
What is anatta?
What is dukkha?
What are the four noble truths?
What did the Buddha teach about suffering?
Why is the idea that 'everything changes' so important to Buddhists?

3   Buddhism today: why learn about Gotama Buddha?

Why do we need to learn about Buddhism in RE?

4 What about **you**? Write down your own reactions to Buddhism.

5 Do you think Siddattha made the right decision? Explain your answer.

Buddha's advice on how to live

The symbol of Buddhism is often shown as a circle with eight sections. It is called the DHAMMACHAKRA. Like the spokes in a wheel or an umbrella, each section of the Dhammachakra needs to be in place to make it work properly. Together, the sections are known as the Eightfold Path.

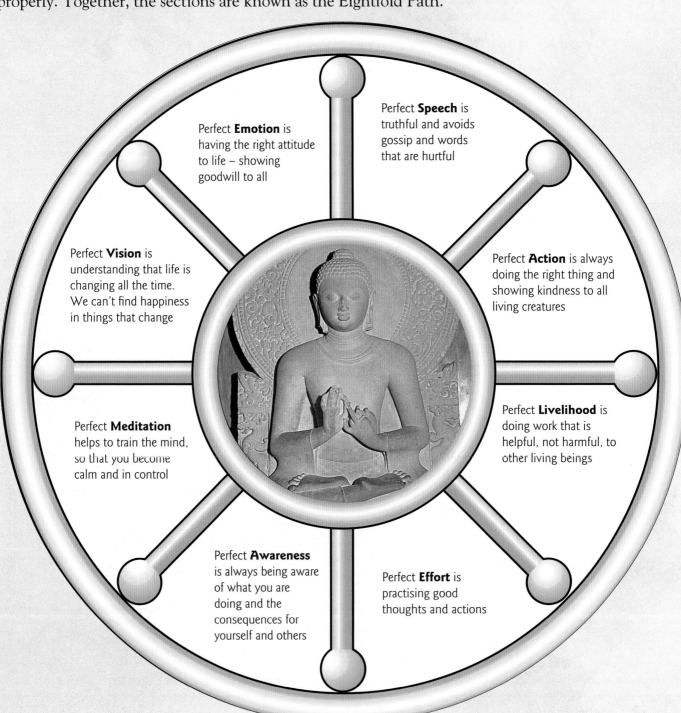

Perfect **Emotion** is having the right attitude to life – showing goodwill to all

Perfect **Speech** is truthful and avoids gossip and words that are hurtful

Perfect **Vision** is understanding that life is changing all the time. We can't find happiness in things that change

Perfect **Action** is always doing the right thing and showing kindness to all living creatures

Perfect **Meditation** helps to train the mind, so that you become calm and in control

Perfect **Livelihood** is doing work that is helpful, not harmful, to other living beings

Perfect **Awareness** is always being aware of what you are doing and the consequences for yourself and others

Perfect **Effort** is practising good thoughts and actions

This photograph shows the sign above the entrance to the London Buddhist Centre. Find the Dhammachakra in the sign.

The centre offers many natural remedies and therapies.

Task

The photographs on this page show one section of the Eightfold Path (Perfect **Livelihood**) being followed by members of a Buddhist community.

1 Take at least one of the other sections and note down the difference it would make:
   a) to you
   b) to your school
   c) to the world
   ... if people followed the teaching of the Buddha.
   For example: Perfect **Speech**. What are the results of verbal bullying, swearing and name calling? How do you feel when someone praises you or speaks kindly to you?

2 What sort of food would be served in the community cafe? Why?

3 Look again at the Eightfold Path. Think of two occupations that would and would not be acceptable to Buddhists, and say why. For example, a Buddhist **would not** work in an abattoir where animals are killed because this would not be Perfect **Action** or Perfect **Livelihood**. A Buddhist **would** work in a hospital because this would be Perfect **Action** and Perfect **Livelihood**.

The centre café.

The garden at the London Buddhist Centre.

6 What is a Buddhist's goal in life?

Religion Buddhism.

Outcomes By the end of this unit you will:

- know what the goal in life is for Buddhists
- understand some ways that help Buddhists to move towards their goal
- understand why meditation is important.

Literacy Select and summarise, read and interpret Buddhist stories, discuss, present ideas in a new way, write an acrostic poem.

Final task Design a leaflet for pupils to use when they visit a Buddhist centre.

This silk collage of lotus flowers hangs in the worship hall at the London Buddhist Centre.

Why the lotus flower?

It is said that the Buddha had a vision of a lotus flower floating on a lake. The lotus flower opened into a beautiful bloom as it reached the sunlight. Its roots were in murky and dark mud. Not every bud reached the sunlight. Some buds stayed closed up. Others opened a little.

● Buddhists are looking for Nirvana

What is Nirvana?

In other religions, people follow a way of life that they believe will lead them to God. Buddhists follow a way of life that trains their minds and leads them to NIRVANA. Nirvana is not a place. It is a way of describing a mind which is happy and at peace.

Reaching Nirvana is difficult. Look at the wall hanging on page 70. Buddhists think that the lotus flower is a symbol of human beings and how they develop. They start in the murky mud, not really understanding life. As they grow in wisdom, they move towards the light, sometimes with a struggle!

How is Nirvana reached?

The Three Jewels

Buddhists practise the Eightfold Path (page 68) to help them to reach Nirvana. The THREE JEWELS, or the Three Refuges, are part of following that Path. They help Buddhists to have Perfect Vision.

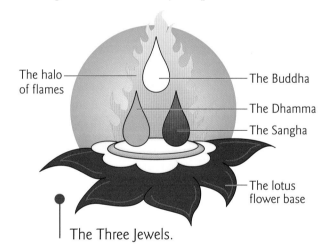

The halo of flames
The Buddha
The Dhamma
The Sangha
The lotus flower base

The Three Jewels.

They are called Jewels because they are very precious. They are also called Refuges because Buddhists believe that they are places to find help and security.

Buddhists will repeat the following words on many occasions, but especially when they are meditating:

I go for refuge to the Buddha;
I go for refuge to the Dhamma;
I go for refuge to the SANGHA.

The Buddha is Gotama Buddha.
The Dhamma is the teachings of the Buddha.
The Sangha is the community of Buddhists.

You will find out more about the Dhamma and the Sangha on pages 72–78.

Task 1

1 Draw a sketch of the lotus flower, labelling the different parts and the ideas they could stand for or symbolise. For example:
   a) Murky and dark water could represent the world with its dangers and difficulties.
   b) What could half-opened buds represent?
   c) What could the sunlight represent?

Task 2

1 Write down three people or things that are most precious to you. Add a note to say how they help you on your pathway of life. For example:
   a) Who makes you laugh?
   b) Who gives you advice?
   c) Who talks to you about your problems?
2 Draft a simple diagram to show the importance of these people or things: your 'jewels'. Add something to your drawing to show that your people or things are important.

● **What are the signposts on the Pathway?**

The Buddha told stories to help his followers understand his teachings, or the Dhamma. The stories on pages 72–75 are examples.

Task 3

In groups, work on one of the three stories. Think about what the story means as you read it. Then decide how you are going to explain the story and its meaning to the rest of the class – by re-telling/role play/drama/poster. Tasks 4, 5 and 6 will help you. The most important thing is that you understand how the Dhamma helps Buddhists to move towards their goal, through an understanding of the Buddha's teaching. This is part of your final task.

The Wagon of Life

Whilst out on a walk, two children came across a small farmhouse, completely surrounded by piles of cartwheels. Curious, they asked the farmer why there were so many and what was to be done with them. The farmer took them to the back of the farmhouse where they saw many carts in the process of repair.

'I mend the carts,' the farmer said, 'for those on the journey of life. The carts have broken because people have piled too many things in them.'

That answer puzzled the children.

The farmer explained. 'Each of these wagons has four wheels. The first is the wheel of bodily needs, such as food, clothing and warmth. The second wheel is love. It is made up of two halves, loving and being loved. The third wheel is goals in life, the things people want to achieve or to own. The fourth wheel is the search for truth and understanding.'

Task 4

1 If you were one of the children, how would you answer the farmer's question? You could answer it by drawing a wagon and labelling the parts with notes to show their meaning. Look back at the story to do this. Be sure to include the wheels, the cart laden with possessions and the pathway.

2 a) Make a list of things you desperately wanted five years ago.

b) Why do you think possessions are so important to people? Write a sentence to show what you think of the storyteller's example of the see-saw showing balance in our lives.

'Why are so many of the carts broken?' asked the children.

'It is because people try to pile up their carts with so many things they think they need. They seem to think that they must always be adding to their possessions. In the end, they overload and break their carts,' said the farmer sadly.

'Can they be repaired?'

'Not always. The wheels of health and love can be difficult to make strong again.'

The children were quiet for a while. Then they asked, 'Why do people think they need more and more things?'

'It is because they haven't realised that happiness is like a game of see-saw. A see-saw only works well when there is a balance. If what you want is heavier than what you have, then you are in a low position and are unhappy. If what you want is less than what you have, then you will be in a high position and more content.

'These broken wagons were overloaded. This prevented them from travelling to their destination. They fell apart. If the owners of the carts had got rid of their load, they would have made much better progress on their journey.'

Turning to the children, the farmer asked, 'So what have you learned from your visit to my farmhouse?'

Weeds and Flowers

Task 5

Think of the weeds as bad thoughts and feelings and the flowers as good thoughts and feelings.

I Work out the meaning of the story. What advice is being given?
  This might help:
'What you must do with darkness is to fill it with light and the darkness simply disappears, like lighting a lantern when evening falls.'

There were two gardens. In one, the gardener was frowning and grumbling. There weren't many flowers. His whole life was spent pulling up weeds. As fast as he pulled them up, they kept coming back. Gardening made him miserable. He didn't have time to enjoy life.

In the other garden, the gardener sat smiling in the sunshine. His garden used to be like the other one but now it was covered in flowers.

The secret?

The second gardener had discovered which flowers did not give the weeds room to grow. These flowers re-seeded themselves and eventually there was no space for the weeds at all!

Kisagotami and her Baby

Kisagotami was the oldest daughter of the poorest man in the village. She was a frail, delicate girl, often ill, not fit for the long hard hours of work that kept her sisters busy. The neighbours were certain that she would never find a husband. But the beauty of her long, dark hair and deep, shining eyes won the heart of a stranger and Kisagotami left the village to join the family of her new husband. They treated her harshly because she was poor and tired easily under her burden of work. But all that changed when Kisagotami gave birth to the first son in her new family. Kisagotami delighted in her child. He was the joy of her life. Motherhood, too, brought respect and care from her relatives. Kisagotami had never known such happiness.

The boy grew strong and graceful. Then one day, at play in the forest, a snake bit him on the ankle. Within hours, Kisagotami and all her household were plunged into mourning. Her dearest was dead. Kisagotami was distraught with grief. She would not eat or sleep. She wandered, like a wild thing, round the houses in the village, cradling the body and pleading at every door for medicine to make her child well again. Her cries frightened the village. 'Whoever heard of medicine for the dead?' they muttered.

But Kisagotami's grief moved the heart of one person in the village. He was an old man, a follower of Gotama, the Buddha. Gently, he advised that Gotama was teaching in the next village. He might be able to give her medicine for her dead child.

That evening, Kisagotami started on her journey. All night she walked, carrying the child. She arrived at midday to find a large crowd gathered around Gotama. She pushed her way through and laid her child on the ground before him. A deep silence fell on the crowd.

'Exalted One,' she pleaded, 'give me medicine for my child.' Gotama gently gathered Kisagotami in his arms. 'Go to the city,' he told her. 'Visit every house. Bring me back a grain of mustard seed from every house that death has not visited. I shall wait for your return.'

Delight filled Kisagotami. At last, someone was listening. Here was one who would help. Through the city she wandered, knocking on every door, pleading for a grain of mustard seed if death had not entered there. She found herself listening to countless stories of sadness, the deaths of wives and husbands, parents and children; stories of old age and sickness. In every house the story was different but the grief was the same, like Kisagotami's own grief. So Kisagotami learned compassion.

At length, she returned to seek Gotama. She found him waiting. She opened her empty hands. Neither spoke. Together they lifted the body of the child and carried him to the cremation ground.

Maurice Lynch.

Task 6

1 List the turning points in this story. Next to each turning point, describe Kisagotami's thoughts and feelings. Choose at least four changes or turning points, but make sure you include the moment when she understood what the Buddha had been trying to teach her.

2 Think about the Buddha's advice to her.

a) Why didn't the Buddha just tell her that death can't be escaped? Write down the reason why it was important for her to find out for herself.

b) Add a sentence to show what you think of this.

75

● **From the buzz of the fire station to silence and calm: the Sangha**

The photograph below shows a centre for Buddhism in London. Buddhism is a world religion which in recent years has spread from countries like Japan, Thailand and Sri Lanka to the United States, Australia and Europe. There are different branches of Buddhism. This centre is for members of the Western Buddhist Order who try to follow Buddhist practice in a way that suits the modern western world.

Once a fire station, this building now has meditation halls, offices, a library, study rooms and a charity shop. Some members of the Western Buddhist Order live here.

As you leave the busy, noisy London road behind, you find peace, calm and quiet inside, and in the garden at the back.

This building is at the heart of the local Buddhist community, the Sangha.

London Buddhist Centre, Bethnal Green.

Task 7

Imagine you are going to send a postcard of the centre to a firefighter who used to work on the premises before its use was changed. Explain what you think would surprise them if they came back now.

● Why is the Sangha important?

> The most important single element in my life as a Buddhist has been my experience of the Sangha – friendship and fellowship with other practising Buddhists.

> The Sangha is where you develop spiritual friendship with others.

> Members of the Sangha give each other help and advice. They also worship and work together as a community.

The members of the Sangha help and support each other in following the Eightfold Path. Remember what they say, and think about it, as this will help with the final task.

Why do people become Buddhists and join the Sangha?

Santavajri, whose story is on page 78.

This shop, where Santavajri works, is called Evolution because it reminds Buddhists that people and things evolve, or change, just as the world does.

77

The story of Santavajri

Up to the age of twenty-seven, I thought I had it all. I had achieved what most people would say was success in my life. I had been to university and had a career as a teacher. I had travelled and lived abroad. I owned my own flat. I could choose what to do with my life. And yet...

I had this feeling that there must be more to life. I couldn't honestly say I was happy. I was some of the time, but other times I was miserable. Life was quite stressful.

I was interested in meditation and decided to sign up for a course at the Centre. I wanted to have a more positive attitude to life and to myself. I found meditation very helpful, and became more interested in Buddhism.

The Buddha's teaching made a lot of sense to me. Especially the idea that what we become is up to us, not God. I had always found it hard to have faith in a God. Buddhism gave me what I was looking for – a religion that didn't ask me to accept something I didn't believe in.

First of all, I decided to become what is called a 'friend' of the Western Buddhist Order. Now I have taken the step of becoming ordained. It means I have made a life-long commitment to the Buddhist Pathway. The teachings of Buddhism are at the centre of my life. I meditate every day. I am a VEGETARIAN and try to live a good life. It really helps to be part of the Sangha. You get support and advice as well as friendship. I live in the Centre's accommodation.

I work in a gift shop called Evolution. It sells goods from developing countries where we know the workers are treated well and where our money goes into projects to improve their lives. In the shop we work as a team and try to treat all our customers in a friendly way. This is all part of following the Pathway. I don't get a wage as such. I am given what I think I need. This is very different from my old way of life. But I am much happier now.'

Task 8

1 How has Santavajri's life changed? Complete a copy of this chart:

Before	Now
Owned a flat	*Lives in Centre's accommodation*
Was a teacher	
Earned money to spend on what she wanted	
Often felt stressed with life	
Didn't feel good about herself	
Wasn't sure if she believed in God or not	
Ate all kinds of food, including meat	

2 Imagine you are going to interview Santavajri. With a partner, prepare some questions about Buddhism and her new life.

How are you expected to behave in Buddhism?

Buddhists don't have any strict rules about how to behave, but they believe there are some ways to be a better person. These ways are called the FIVE PRECEPTS. They help to guide Buddhists on the Eightfold Path (Perfect Action). These Five Precepts show good and bad behaviour so that Buddhists know which path to follow.

The Five Precepts

Behaviour to avoid	Behaviour to encourage
Intent to harm any living thing or person	Acts and thoughts of loving kindness
Taking anything that is not given	Generosity and honesty
Abusing your body in sexual misconduct	Living contentedly and calmly
Speaking in ways that hurt or offend others	Speaking the truth and using what you say for the good of others
Using drink or drugs that make you lose control or confuse your thinking	Keeping a clear mind so that your deeds and actions are under your control

If you follow these precepts, then it will affect everything you do.

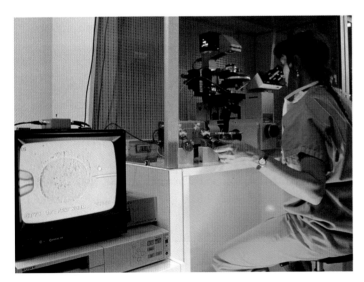

This is how one scientist described the effect on her career when she put the precepts into practice:

'I have always worked in scientific fields including atomic energy research. Because Buddhism is based upon non-harming, I could no longer be involved with atomic energy research because of the possibility of making destructive weapons and the real dangers to the environment.'

Instead, she uses her scientific knowledge and skill in areas of science that help people, such as monitoring the developments of unborn babies and detecting cancer in women.

Task 9

Think of two examples of a bad habit and then note down how anyone could change it for the better. For example:

Bad habit	How to change
Arguing with the referee.	Count to ten before speaking!
Always leaving homework to the last minute.	Plan your time better.

What does a place for Buddhist meditation look like?

Buddhists do not worship in the sense of worshipping God. There is no God in Buddhism. Meditation helps them to focus on values that are good and worthwhile. It helps them to follow the Eightfold Path.

Because there are different groups of Buddhists, their places for meditation don't all look exactly the same. Some are plainer than others. But there are things that they all have in common.

There will be a statue of the Buddha (called a Buddharupa). Usually there will be flowers, candles and incense. The atmosphere will be calm and quiet so that meditation is not disturbed.

Before meditation begins, Buddhists may recite this poem:

A shrine built under a Bodhi tree in Thailand.

> Reverencing the Buddha, we offer flowers:
> Flowers that today are fresh and sweetly blooming,
> Flowers that tomorrow are faded and fallen.
> Our bodies too, like flowers, will fade away.
>
> Reverencing the Buddha, we offer candles:
> To him, who is the light, we offer light.
> From his greater lamp a lesser lamp we light within us,
> The lamp of Bodhi shining within our hearts.
>
> Reverencing the Buddha, we offer incense:
> Incense whose fragrance pervades the air.
> The fragrance of the perfect life, sweeter than incense,
> Spreads in all directions around the world.

Task 10

This section on the Buddha and meditation is important for your final task.

Flowers, candles and incense help Buddhists in their meditation. Each verse of the poem on page 80 tells you something about why. Remember, Bodhi means wisdom.

1 Draw a simple picture illustrating each verse and write down what each item means to the worshippers. Include answers to these questions:
   a) Why does the verse mention that flowers fade?
   b) What is 'sweeter than incense'?
2 Look up the word 'reverence'. What does it tell you about attitudes to the Buddha?

● **What happens in meditation?**

Meditation is about sitting still, shutting out all distractions, and being silent. It is very important to Buddhists and they meditate either on their own or with others.

The following Buddhist meditation is called 'The bringing into being of universal loving kindness'. It helps Buddhists to develop kindness and love for themselves, all living beings and the planet.

Start with yourself – feeling good about yourself and hoping things go well for you.

Focus on someone you like, for example, a friend, hoping that everything goes well for this friend and that they are happy.

Think of someone you know but not very well. Extend your feelings of loving kindness to them.

Think kindly of someone with whom you've had an argument or whom you dislike.

Finally, include in your loving feelings the wider world, every living being.

Task 11

In an acrostic poem, the first letters of each line spell out a word that shows the subject of the poem. For example:

Catches mice, at least, he tries to,
Affectionate, especially when hungry,
Tigger is the best cat in the world!

Write your own acrostic poem, using MEDITATION or SILENCE as the starting point, to show what these two words mean for Buddhists.

● How do Buddhists see the end of their lives?

A Buddhist's aim is to reach Nirvana. Nirvana describes a state of mind that is wise, happy and at peace. Nirvana is reached by following the Eightfold Path. This is helped by:

- the Three Jewels (page 71).
- the advice given in the Five Precepts (page 79).
- meditation (pages 80–81).

Reaching Nirvana is difficult, like the lotus flower finding its way through the muddy water to the light. It may take many lifetimes. This is about rebirth. Think of it like this:

The light started with the first candle. Before it was finished, its flame was used to light the second. Before the second is finished, its flame will be used to light the third candle, and so on. It is not the same flame, nor is it completely different. Without the flame from the first, the others would not be alight. It is like this with rebirth. You keep on going but as a different person.

When true happiness, wisdom and peace have been reached, that is Nirvana.

Final task

So ... what is a Buddhist's goal in life?

Design a leaflet for school pupils to use when they visit a Buddhist centre. The leaflet should explain how the features and activities at that centre help Buddhists to move closer to their goal.

A

B

C

D

1 Write a label to go with each of Pictures A–D saying what the pictures show.
2 Explain how each picture shows a way in which Buddhists are helped to move closer to their goal. You should include:
   a) What the lotus flower symbolises about growing towards their goal.
   b) Why the Sangha is important.
   c) How Buddhists are helped by meditation and the example of the Buddha.
   d) How the Dhamma brings understanding. Use a story as an example of the Buddha's teaching.
3 What do you think is the most important thing a Buddhist would want you to learn on your visit? In the leaflet, it could be set out like this:

   We hope you have enjoyed your visit to our Centre. If you remember only one thing, this is what we would like it to be...

4 Finally, in your leaflet, respond to the following request from the Buddhist community:

   To help us plan other visits, please write down a question about Buddhism to which you think pupils of your age would like an answer.

7 What are we doing to the environment?

Religions Ideas common to all and examples taken from all.

Outcomes By the end of this unit you will:

- know some reasons why human beings have harmed the environment
- understand some religious beliefs about the environment
- express your own wonders and worries about the environment
- make your own action plan for the environment.

Literacy Summarise, use descriptive language, read and analyse stories, speak and listen in groups.

Final task Make a 'Wonder and Worry Wall' to show your hopes and fears about the environment. Write a personal action plan.

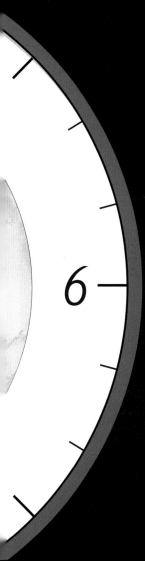

The History of a Day

. . . and then, on the stroke of midnight, people appeared. All through the morning, and the afternoon, they just wandered around in small groups – hunting animals with spears and arrows, sheltering in caves, dressing themselves in skins. At about 18.00 hours they began to learn about seeds and manure, and so on. They started to herd and milk animals. By about 19.30 hours some people, from Egypt to North India, were living in cities.

Moses came and went at about 20.45 hours. Buddha was in India at about 22.10 hours. Jesus was around at 22.30 hours, as also, give a minute or so, were the Great Wall of China and Julius Caesar. Muhammad ﷺ was there at 23.00 hours.

At around 23.30 hours, big cities appeared in northern Europe. From about 23.45 onwards people went out from those cities, exploring their world and taking over some other countries. At about 23.58 hours they had a big war amongst themselves, and then had another big war, only 50 seconds later.

During the last minute before midnight, people invented nuclear weapons; landed on the moon; doubled the world's population; made five hundred species of animals extinct; and used up more oil and metal than in all the previous 23 hours 59 minutes put together.

It was now midnight again. The start of a new day.

Adapted from *Values and Visions* by Sally Burns and Georgeanne Lamont.

Task 1

Talk about 'The History of a Day' with a partner. How does it make you feel? What is the writer trying to say? Jot down your first reactions to it. Keep these notes. You might need them for your final task.

How are humans damaging the environment?

'The History of a Day' carries a rather scary message. Humans have long been able to affect the natural world. They have learnt to control fire and herd animals. But it is only in recent times (in the last few minutes of that 'Day') that humans have had the massive power to change or to damage our whole planet. Look back to the story – what damage have humans been doing according to these writers?

That is only a part of it. There are many other causes for concern.

Task 2

Work in fours, looking at the following examples of environmental problems. Two of you take Example 1, two of you take Example 2.

1 Write your answers to the four questions below. You could use the information on pages 86–87, plus your own knowledge, or you could do further research on the internet.

- What is happening?
- Why is it happening?
- What might be the consequences?
- What's it got to do with me?

2 Report your answers to the other pair.

Example 1: It's getting warmer. Why?

All around the Earth is a blanket of gas, which keeps us alive. This is the Earth's atmosphere. It lets in just the right amount of energy from the Sun for life to exist. It lets out just the right amount of energy to stop us overheating. But the blanket of gas is changing. In particular there is more carbon dioxide (CO_2).

Our atmosphere is now trapping more heat inside and so the Earth is getting warmer. Most scientists believe that this 'greenhouse effect' is one cause of 'global warming'. Global warming could cause the climate to change so there will be more droughts in some places and more floods in others.

Here are some of the reasons why the atmosphere is changing:

- **Power stations** burn oil and coal to make electricity, which releases CO_2 into the atmosphere.
- **Fumes** from factories, cars, lorries and planes add to the effect.
- **Burning rainforest** releases CO_2 just as a power station does but at the same time this gets rid of one of the very things that could help to solve the problem. Trees live off CO_2. They absorb it and turn it back into oxygen. The rainforest acts as the Earth's lung, except that, unlike human lungs, this one breathes in CO_2 and breathes out oxygen.

Example 2: It's a load of rubbish! Why?

In the UK most of the rubbish that you put in your dustbin – your juice can, your crisp packet or your plastic bag – finishes up at a landfill site like the one shown in this photo. The sites are lined and covered with earth to try to stop the POLLUTION from seeping out. Once they are filled up, the sites are then landscaped in an attempt to make them more attractive. But we still don't know the longer-term effects of all this rubbish on the environment.

Why is there so much rubbish?

- In wealthy countries like ours, people are consuming more and more each year.
- We choose highly packaged goods for their appearance and convenience.
- People find it easier to throw things away than to recycle them. Britain recycles less than almost every other country in Europe.
- It is often cheaper to replace broken goods than to repair them.

Task 3

1 In a group, collect pictures to show either the environment at its best or the environment at its worst. You could look in newspapers, magazines or on websites of environmental groups.
2 Make a group decision about which are the five best examples for each category. Paste these ten pictures on to a poster.
3 Agree a group statement about why you have chosen these examples and write this statement underneath your poster.
4 Give a talk to the class, using your poster.

● Why are humans damaging the environment?

To tackle the two problems highlighted on pages 86–87 we need to do more than just worry. We need to understand the bigger problems that lie behind them. Maybe if we could do something about those, then . . .

B | **Technology** has made life better for many people but its effect on the environment has not always been considered.

A | **Population** In 1900, the world population was one billion. In 2000, it was six billion. More people means more demands on the planet.

C | **Consumerism** In the rich countries, people want more comforts and more luxuries. They want different foods and leisure goods. This uses more resources to make them, more factories and lorries and planes to supply them and more rubbish to throw away.

D **Poverty** In many of the poorer countries of the world, people have to harm the environment just to survive. For example, rainforests are cleared so that the land can be used to grow crops to sell to rich countries.

E **Attitudes** People have not thought of the Earth as a very special place to be treasured and respected.

Task 4

Write each of the five reasons (A–E) on a separate card.

a) Look back to pages 86–87. Which of the reasons help to explain the two problems?

b) Arrange the five reasons in a circle round a large sheet of paper. Add lines and make notes to show how these reasons are connected.

c) Put the five reasons in order of priority. Which would you tackle first?

d) Which of them do you think it is easiest to do anything about? Explain your choice.

e) 'We should all just give up and let people do what they want to the environment. There is nothing we can do to make it better.' Write a paragraph to explain whether you agree or disagree with this statement.

How can we change our attitude to the environment?

If the Earth were only a few feet in diameter, floating a few feet above a field somewhere, people would come from everywhere to marvel at it. People would walk around it, marvelling at its big pools of water, its little pools and the water flowing between the pools. People would marvel at the bumps on it and the holes in it, and the different areas on it. And they would marvel at the very thin layer of gas surrounding it and at the water suspended in the gas. People would marvel at all the creatures walking around the surface of the ball, and at the creatures in the water, and at the green vegetation growing on the surface. The people would declare it as SACRED, because it was the only one, and they would protect it so that it would not be hurt. The ball would be the greatest wonder known and people would come to pray to it, to be healed, to gain its knowledge, to know its great beauty, and to defend it with their lives because they would somehow know that their lives, their own roundness, could be nothing without it. If the Earth were only a few feet in diameter.

'If the Earth were small' by Olaf Skarsholt.

Some people have had the kind of experience that Skarsholt talks about.

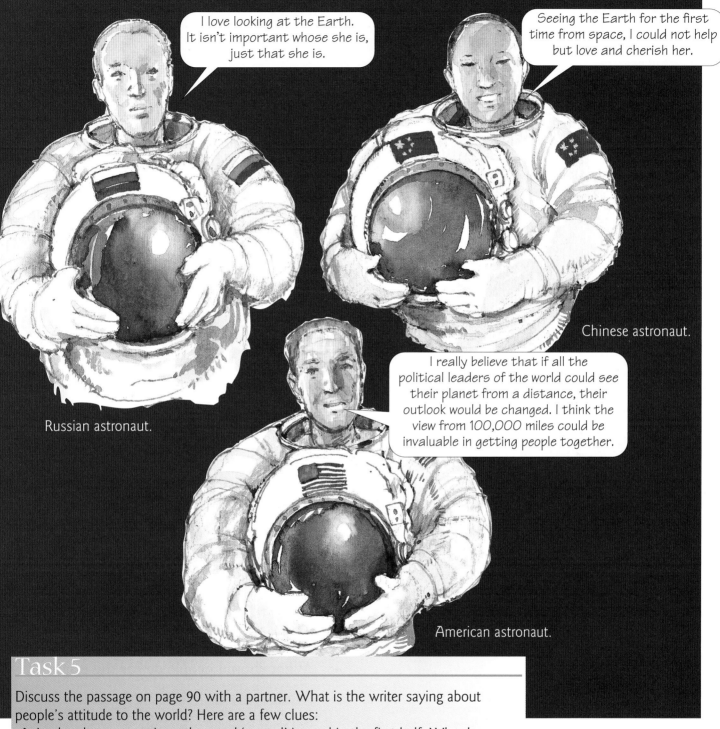

I love looking at the Earth. It isn't important whose she is, just that she is.

Seeing the Earth for the first time from space, I could not help but love and cherish her.

Chinese astronaut.

Russian astronaut.

I really believe that if all the political leaders of the world could see their planet from a distance, their outlook would be changed. I think the view from 100,000 miles could be invaluable in getting people together.

American astronaut.

Task 5

Discuss the passage on page 90 with a partner. What is the writer saying about people's attitude to the world? Here are a few clues:

a) Look at how many times the word 'marvel' is used in the first half. Why do you think this is?

b) Write the word 'sacred' in the centre of a large piece of paper. Write around it any other phrases, words or features used by the author that show the earth is sacred, for example: 'people would come to pray to it'.

Task 6

In pairs, choose four sayings each from F–M.

a) Answer, in one sentence, the question that follows each saying.

b) Share your answers with your partner.

Keep your answers for stage 2 of the final task.

● Can religion help us to change our attitude?

Some people think a religious viewpoint is also very important. On pages 92–93 are eight different religious sayings about the environment and how we should treat it.

F

A wise rabbi was walking along a road when he saw a man planting a tree. The rabbi asked him, 'How many years will it take for this tree to bear fruit?' The man answered that it would take seventy years. The rabbi asked, 'Are you so fit and strong that you expect to live that long and eat its fruit?' The man answered, 'I found a fruitful world because my ancestors planted for me. So I will do the same for my children.'

A Jewish tale.

Why was the man planting the tree?

G

When I look up at your heavens, the work of your fingers,
At the moon and the stars you have set in place.
What is frail mortal, that you should be mindful of him,
A human being, that you should notice him?
Yet you have made him little less than a god,
Crowning his head with glory and honour.
You make him master over all that you have made,
Putting everything in subjection under his feet.
All sheep and oxen, all the wild beasts,
And everything that moves along ocean paths.
Lord, our sovereign,
How glorious is your name throughout the world.

Psalm 8, a song from the Bible that is important to both Christians and Jews.

What did the writer of Psalm 8 think was so amazing about God?

H

If a Muslim plants a tree or sows a field, and men and beasts and birds eat from it, all of it is charity on his part.
The world is green and beautiful and God has appointed you his stewards over it.

Words of the prophet Muhammad .
A steward is someone who looks after or is trusted to care for something.

What should people do for the earth?

I

Just as with her own life a mother shields from hurt her own, her only child – let there be love for all the universe in all its heights and depths and breadth.

A Buddhist meditation.

How should we feel about the environment?

J

God lives in every corner of existence. Therefore the whole creation is sacred.

From Hindu sacred writings.

Why should we look after the environment?

K

By God's will the Lord has created the creation and watches over all.
God's light pervades all creation.

From Sikh sacred writings.

Where can we find God?

L

This we know: the Earth does not belong to man, man belongs to the Earth. All things are connected like the blood that connects us all. Man did not weave the web of life, he is merely a strand of it. Whatever he does to the web, he does to himself.

Chief Seattle in a letter to the US President, 1855. Native Americans believe in spiritual forces which bind every part of nature together – land, animals and people.

Why is the earth important to humans?

M

The planet is a gift from God and therefore not to be exploited. We must be aware of the consequences of our actions.

Pope John Paul II.

Why should we take care of the environment?

Task 7

Match each of the sayings (F–M) to one of these key ideas.

a) Celebration – the environment is so amazing it should fill us with worship and wonder.

b) INTERDEPENDENCE – all parts of the environment (including us) are connected and we should live as if we are interdependent.

c) STEWARDSHIP – we are given responsibility to care for the Earth for coming generations, so they can enjoy it.

● **What can we do about the environment?**

In the last minute of 'The History of a Day' (see page 85), in its final seconds, people have begun to realise what is happening to the environment. Many non-religious groups (such as the World Wide Fund for Nature, Friends of the Earth and Greenpeace) have led the way in trying to protect the environment and protesting against those who damage it. Many religious groups, such as Christian Aid, CAFOD (Catholic Agency for Overseas Development) and the Tear Fund, Islamic Relief and Tzedek, have also campaigned to protect the environment as part of their campaign against poverty. Some religious people feel that protecting the environment is the most important issue facing our times.

Example 1: The Chipko movement

In 1730, in the Rajasthan region of India, a local ruler wanted to chop down trees as fuel for his kilns. He sent his men with their axes to an area where a group of Hindus had taken a vow never to take life. This included life in the natural world and especially trees. Because they also believed in non-violence, they would not fight. As the woodcutters and soldiers arrived, the people – 363 men, women and children – hugged their trees to protect them. They were all killed.

This story inspired a group of women to start the Chipko movement in 1973. It still uses a form of non-violent struggle. 'Chipko' comes from a word meaning embrace and the women link hands around trees to prevent them from being felled.

A supporter of the Chipko movement.

Task 8

Environmental groups often have symbols that show what they believe in.

Draw a symbol for the Chipko movement that shows their key beliefs.

94

Example 2: Ten environmental commandments

In the 1980s, some young Jews and Christians wrote these ten environmental commandments.

1 I am the Lord your God who has created heaven and earth. Know that you are my partners in creation; therefore, take care of the air, water, earth, plants and animals, as if they were your brothers and sisters.

2 Know that in giving you life, I have given you responsibility, freedom and limited resources.

3 Steal not from the future; honour your children by giving them a chance of long life.

4 Implant in your children a love of nature.

5 Remember that humanity can use technology, but cannot recreate life that has been destroyed.

6 Set up pressure groups to prevent future catastrophes.

7 Throw out all arms which destroy for ever the foundations of life.

8 Be self-disciplined in the small details of your life.

9 Set aside time in your weekly day of rest to be with the world rather than to use the world.

10 Remember that you are not the owner of the land, just its guardian.

Task 9

1 Look at the eighth commandment. Make a list of ways in which you can be 'self-disciplined in the small details of your life' so that you help the environment. For example, turning off lights when they're not needed.

2 The words 'responsibility', 'freedom' and 'limited resources' are used in the second commandment. Look up these words in a dictionary. In your own words, explain what the second commandment means.

3 With a partner, choose three commandments which you think are particularly important if the future is going to be any better than the past for the environment. You could look back to pages 88–89 where you examined causes of environmental problems.

Final task

So ... what are we doing to the environment?
Stage 1: Make a Wonder and Worry Wall

Wonder will describe feelings of amazement at the beauty of the world.

Worry will express anxieties about what is happening to the world.

Look back through the unit and show your response to what you have learned by making a list of words that describe your feelings about the earth.

For example: beauty
                threatened

Organise all your words in columns headed **Wonder** and **Worry**. Pick two words from Wonder and two words from Worry and write a sentence for each to explain why you chose them.

As a class, you could write your words on sticky labels or Post-its and make a Wonder and Worry Wall of the labels to go with the title: 'The world is...'

Your sentences could be added to the display. What about word processing them?

Stage 2: Draw up an action plan

Remember 'The History of a Day' (page 85)? We have now started the new day. We can't put the clock back! But we can still take action. The future is ours. What can we do to make sure that the future for the environment is better than the recent past? And how can religion help us?

1   Think back to the work you have done in this unit.
   a) List four mistakes that have been made in the past that should not be repeated.
   b) List four things that human beings need to do before time runs out.

2 a) Choose three religious ideas from this unit that you think are particularly helpful in encouraging people to respect the environment. Look back at the quotes on pages 92 and 93.
   b) Choose just one idea from **a)** then write a paragraph about how this religious idea you have chosen is relevant. Be specific! How might this idea
      • change people's attitudes
      • encourage them to take action

3   Here is a Native American story:

Once there was a great forest fire, and all the animals and birds rushed to escape. Hummingbird went to the river, and collected a drop of water. The other birds laughed. 'What are you doing?' they asked. She replied, 'I'm doing what I can.'

List two things that you can do to help. What would be your drops of water?

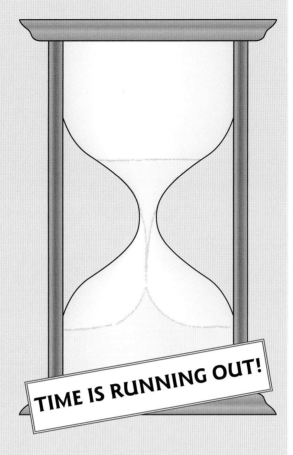

TIME IS RUNNING OUT!

Many religious believers trace their beliefs about the environment back to the creation stories. You are going to look at two stories from different traditions.

The Jewish and Christian story of creation

Nothing. Nothing to see. Nothing to hear. Nothing to touch. Nothing to taste. Nothing to smell. Just nothing.

But God. Not seeing. Not hearing. Not touching. Not tasting. Not smelling. Just being.

And from being, God makes everything. The sky, the earth, the water. Everything. The Earth is totally empty and the water is totally dark but the Spirit of God sweeps across the water.

Light appears to give life. Light and dark drift apart as they do every day when day turns to night and night turns to day. This evening and this morning make the first day.

A huge space appears in the middle of the water and the water runs below it and above it. The water below becomes the sea and the water above becomes the sky that carries rain. This evening and this morning make a second day.

The waters below the sky come together so that dry land appears, the Earth where we live. All kinds of plants sprout on the Earth – luscious fruit trees, fragrant flowers, waving ears of corn . . . This evening and this morning make a third day.

Light appears in the sky, separating day and night, and marking days and years. And then two great light-givers. The bigger light, the Sun, shines in the day and the smaller light, the Moon, shines at night. Stars also appear. This evening and this morning make a fourth day.

All kinds of creatures appear in the sky and the sea – birds and insects, fish and reptiles … They spread across the sky and the sea and more and more of them appear until the sky and sea fill up with

them. This evening and this morning make a fifth day.

All kinds of animals appear on the Earth – lions and bears, cattle and sheep, squirrels and rats . . . Then come the people, on the same day. They are like the animals in so many ways but like God, too. The people have God's image in them and are filled with God's blessing. They spread and grow. They are given all the birds, fish and animals. They are in charge of them and need to care for them. And, for God, this is all very good. This evening and this morning make a sixth day.

Now there is light and darkness, sky, earth, and sea, plants and trees, fishes and birds, animals and people. There is just one more thing that the world needs for creation to be complete – peaceful rest. It is a special day, the seventh day, and God blesses it and makes it holy.

'Nothing and Everything' from *Creation Stories* by Angela Wood.

A Hindu creation story

Many stories are told of the cycle of life, but let me explain it to you like this. This is not the first world, nor is it the first universe. There have been, and will be, many more worlds and universes than there are drops of water in the holy river Ganges.

The universes are made by Lord Brahma, the creator. They are looked after by Lord Vishnu. They are destroyed by Lord Shiva. From the destruction comes new life, so Lord Shiva is the Destroyer and the Re-creator.

How long is the universe? Its length is beyond imagination. One day to Lord Brahma is longer than four thousand million of our years. When the Lord Brahma of this universe has lived a lifetime of such days, the universe is completely destroyed by Lord Shiva.

Then for an unimaginable period of time, chaos and water alone exist. Then once again, Lord Vishnu appears, floating on the vast ocean, resting on the great serpent Ananta. From his navel springs a lotus flower and from this comes Lord Brahma – and the cycle begins again.

Vishnu appears, resting on the great serpent Ananta, floating on the cosmic ocean. From his navel comes Brahma, the creator.

Task

These stories were spoken and written down long before modern scientists told us what the world is like and how things happen. Some people say that modern science has made these stories irrelevant. Others say that these stories still teach us important things about the Earth and the human responsibility to look after it.

1 Make a list of at least three differences between the Jewish/Christian story and the Hindu story. Think about:
   a) Who is the creator?
   b) What do they create?
   c) How long do they take to create?

2 Find some words or phrases in the stories showing that the writer thought that
   a) the Earth was a wonderful and mysterious place
   b) humans were expected to care for the earth
   c) all parts of creation fit carefully together.

3 One story suggests that creation is a one-off event, the other that creation will happen again and again. Which is which?

4 Which view is closer to your own? Write a sentence to explain your choice. If neither is close, then write a paragraph to explain your own view.

Song of the battery hen

We can't grumble about accommodation:
we have a new concrete floor that's
always dry, four walls that are
painted white, and a sheet-iron roof
the rain drums on. A fan blows warm air
beneath our feet to disperse the smell
of chicken-shit and, on dull days,
fluorescent lighting sees us.

You can tell me: if you come by
the north door, I am in the twelfth pen,
on the left-hand side of the third row
from the floor; and in that pen
I am usually the middle one of three.
But, even without directions, you'd
discover me. I have the same orange-
red comb, yellow beak and auburn
feathers, but as the door opens and you
hear above the electric fan a kind of
one-word wail, I am the one
who sounds loudest in my head.

Listen. Outside this house there's an
orchard with small moss-green apple
trees; beyond that, two fields of
cabbages; then, on the far side of
the road, a broiler house. Listen:
one cockerel crows out of there, as
tall and proud as the first hour of sun.
Sometimes I stop calling with the others
to listen, and wonder if he hears me.

The next time you come here, look for me.
Notice the way I sound inside my head.
God made us all quite differently,
and blessed us with this expensive home.

Edwin Brock.

Religions Hinduism and
Judaism as case studies.

Outcomes By the end of
this unit you will:

* find out why some people
  are vegetarian and others
  are not
* find out whether being
  religious affects your
  views about animals.

Literacy Read and
discuss a poem, analyse
sacred texts, organise notes
for a group presentation,
write a paragraph,
meditation, poem or prayer.

Final task Group
presentation and a personal
response.

Task 1

1 Is the hen trying to tell us something in this poem? What does she really mean?
2 How does this writer want you to feel about battery hens? How do you know?
3 Working in pairs, write down any features of this poem which let you know what
   the writer feels.

● Why produce chicken this way?

Much modern chicken farming is done in 'factory farms' – like a factory because a raw material (bird-feed) goes in one end and a product (eggs or chicken pieces) comes out the other end. It is an efficient business, but it arouses strong feelings in some people and a variety of opinions.

It makes chicken and eggs cheap in the shops, so poorer people can enjoy them.

It's a way of producing more food, so more people can be fed.

The meat is low in fat, so leads to healthy eating.

It's selfish – why should animals suffer just to give us cheap food?

It's unnatural – for example, the hens have no space to run around in and no natural light.

It's degrading – all living beings should be treated with respect. These chickens are treated as machines in a manufacturing process.

It's carefully controlled by inspectors who make sure that the hens are treated well.

Task 2

In your final task you will be trying to write a balanced account of this issue. These notes will help you to prepare for it.

1 Look at the eight opinions here. Sort them into arguments for and against factory farming. Record them on a table like this:

Arguments for	Arguments against

2 Add other arguments that you can think of on both sides.
3 Does it matter to you that much of the chicken and eggs we eat are produced in this way? Note down your own personal view. Give reasons for your opinion.

It's cruel – the birds are cramped together and they peck each other. Many show signs of distress.

● Why are some religious people vegetarian?

When it is unclear or debatable what is right and what is wrong in a situation, it is called a MORAL DILEMMA. There are many moral dilemmas surrounding the treatment of animals. Factory farming is just one of them. This unit will concentrate on two such dilemmas – vegetarianism and VIVISECTION.

A vegetarian is someone who does not eat meat, fish or any product made from animal slaughter. Some vegetarians (called vegans) go further than that and refuse to eat any other products from animals such as milk and eggs.

People have different reasons for being vegetarian:

- Principle – they think that eating meat is wrong for religious or other reasons.
- Taste – they don't like the taste of meat.
- Health – they think that meat is unhealthy.

All religions are against cruelty to animals, in that they generally promote kindness and understanding between all living creatures. However, their definitions of cruelty vary considerably. People from different religions and even within the same religion often disagree about vegetarianism. You will examine one religion where vegetarianism is important and one where it is left to individual choice.

Case study 1: Why are most Hindus vegetarian?

Hindus believe in:

AHIMSA Every living thing is sacred. The supreme spirit of Brahman is in everything.

REINCARNATION When someone dies, their soul or spirit is reborn in another living form (including animals). This new life will be based on how the person has lived their present life. So, animals have a spirit or soul.

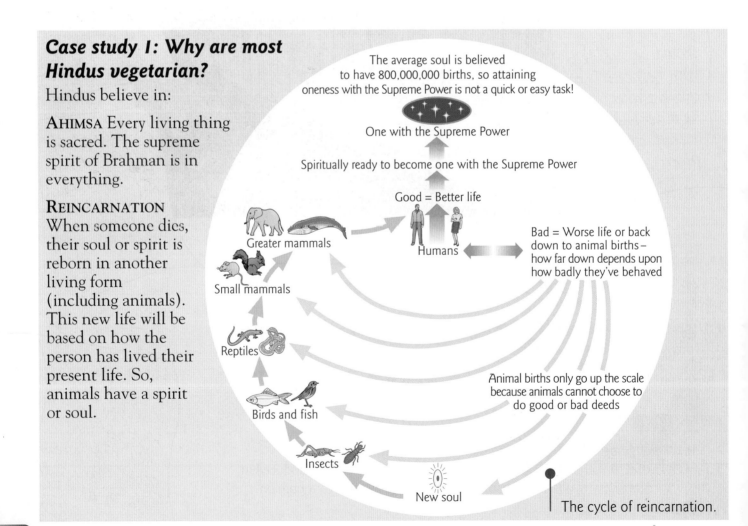

The average soul is believed to have 800,000,000 births, so attaining oneness with the Supreme Power is not a quick or easy task!

One with the Supreme Power

Spiritually ready to become one with the Supreme Power

Good = Better life

Bad = Worse life or back down to animal births – how far down depends upon how badly they've behaved

Greater mammals

Small mammals

Reptiles

Birds and fish

Insects

New soul

Humans

Animal births only go up the scale because animals cannot choose to do good or bad deeds

The cycle of reincarnation.

He is God, hidden in all things, their inmost soul who is in all. He watches the works of creation, lives in all things, watches all things.

Svetasvatara Upanishad.

Meat cannot be obtained without harming living creatures . . . shun the meat.

The Vedas.

A householder should regard deer, camels, donkeys, mice, snakes, birds and bees as his sons; for what difference is there between his sons and them?

Bhagavata Purana.

Within Hinduism, cows are treated with particularly great respect and should not be killed. You can find out more about this on pages 110–113.

Every living creature is the son of the Supreme Lord and he does not tolerate even an ant being killed ... A human being has no need to kill animals because God has supplied so many nice things ... Of all kinds of animal killing, the killing of cows is the most vicious because the cow gives us all kinds of pleasure by supplying milk.

Bhagavad Gita.

Task 3

1 Using all the information here, work out three reasons why most Hindus are vegetarian and would probably never eat beef. Note down which is the strongest of your three reasons. This will help with the final task.

2 In a group, discuss the following questions. What do you think about the Hindu belief that animals and humans have a spirit or soul that is reborn when their body dies (reincarnation)? If you did believe this, how would it change your life now? For example, would you be a vegetarian? Why?

Case study 2: How do Jews decide about vegetarianism?

Judaism has some strict rules on food. There are instructions about what food can be eaten, laws about what food can be combined with another. Jews are forbidden to eat pork. It is a very food-conscious religion. But on the issue of vegetarianism, it is up to the individual to decide.

Here are extracts from two different Jewish websites:

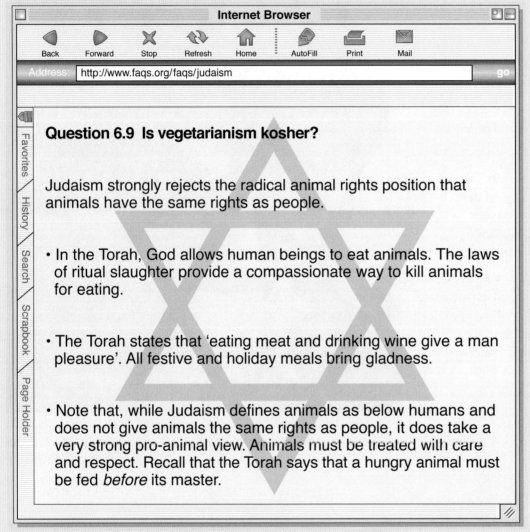

Internet Browser

Back   Forward   Stop   Refresh   Home   AutoFill   Print   Mail

Address: http://www.faqs.org/faqs/judaism   go

Favorites History Search Scrapbook Page Holder

Question 6.9 Is vegetarianism kosher?

Judaism strongly rejects the radical animal rights position that animals have the same rights as people.

- In the Torah, God allows human beings to eat animals. The laws of ritual slaughter provide a compassionate way to kill animals for eating.

- The Torah states that 'eating meat and drinking wine give a man pleasure'. All festive and holiday meals bring gladness.

- Note that, while Judaism defines animals as below humans and does not give animals the same rights as people, it does take a very strong pro-animal view. Animals must be treated with care and respect. Recall that the Torah says that a hungry animal must be fed *before* its master.

Adapted from www.faqs.org/faqs/judaism

But it says here that...

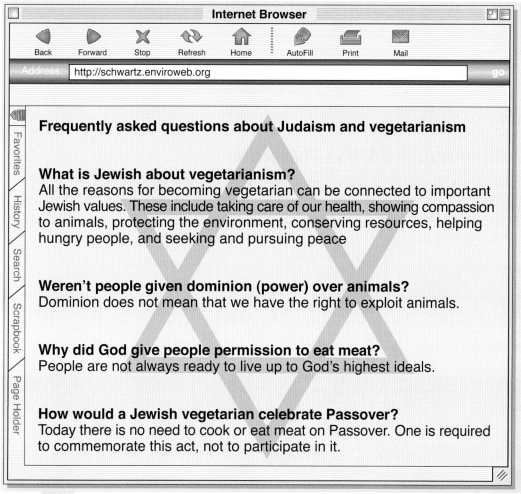

Internet Browser

Back Forward Stop Refresh Home AutoFill Print Mail

Address: http://schwartz.enviroweb.org   go

Frequently asked questions about Judaism and vegetarianism

What is Jewish about vegetarianism?
All the reasons for becoming vegetarian can be connected to important Jewish values. These include taking care of our health, showing compassion to animals, protecting the environment, conserving resources, helping hungry people, and seeking and pursuing peace

Weren't people given dominion (power) over animals?
Dominion does not mean that we have the right to exploit animals.

Why did God give people permission to eat meat?
People are not always ready to live up to God's highest ideals.

How would a Jewish vegetarian celebrate Passover?
Today there is no need to cook or eat meat on Passover. One is required to commemorate this act, not to participate in it.

Adapted from http://schwartz.enviroweb.org
The full FAQ page has 38 questions and answers.

Task 4

I Copy and complete these two 'word bubbles'. Use any of the ideas in the two websites. Try to find at least two reasons each person could use.

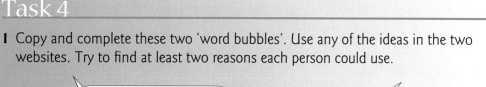

As a Jew I am a vegetarian because ...

As a Jew I eat meat because ...

2 Which do you think is the strongest argument? Give reasons. In your answer refer to the sources on pages 104–105.
3 Some of the arguments are religious ones, some are not. Make two lists: one of religious arguments, one of other arguments.
4 Find examples of the following:
   a) references to the Torah (the most sacred text of Judaism)
   b) appealing to conscience.

● Vivisection and other issues

By now you should have a good idea about how Hindus and Jews feel about using animals for food. Another issue about animals which arouses strong feelings is vivisection. Vivisection is the use of live animals for scientific research, for example, in testing new drugs or researching into the effects of disease.

Arguments AGAINST vivisection

a) It's selfish. Some diseases are our fault, for example, when smokers get lung cancer. Why should animals be killed to find cures for something that is our fault?

b) It's unreliable. A drug may work when it is tested on an animal, but that does not mean it will work on a human.

c) It's unnecessary. We could make much greater use of computer technology to model human organs.

d) It's cruel. Even though rules are followed, that does not mean that innocent creatures do not suffer pain and stress.

e) It's against God's will. Animals are part of God's creation too.

Mammals such as rats, mice and rabbits are routinely used in experiments. The usefulness of these experiments is the subject of ongoing debate.

Arguments FOR vivisection

f) It's rare. Look at how little we use animals for experiments!

g) It brings massive benefits to humans. We now have much healthier and safer lives than our grandparents. We expect things we buy to be safe. They have to be tested. This includes animal testing. Diabetes can only be controlled because of animal research.

h) It's carefully controlled. There are government rules that have to be followed when using animals.

i) It's necessary. You need a whole body to experiment on – you can't just use body cells or tissues.

j) It's within God's will. God gave us the skill to find ways of making our lives better.

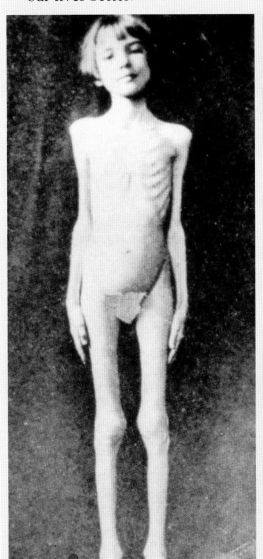 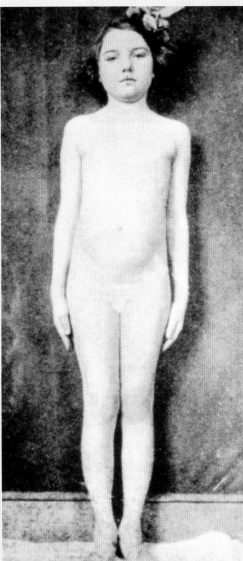

These photos show a girl who suffered from diabetes (left) and how she improved with the help of insulin (right). She was one of the first people to be treated with insulin, which was extracted from slaughtered cattle.

Task 5

Discuss arguments **a)** to **j)** with a partner.

1 Which is the strongest argument FOR and which is the strongest argument AGAINST vivisection? Note down your choice, and give your reasons.

2 Look back to what you have found out about Hindu and Jewish teaching on how to treat animals. Note down any aspect of that teaching which you think could be applied to vivisection.

3 Discuss your ideas in a group and note down any extra points. These will all help with the final task.

4 As a group, put together any questions you wish to ask to find out more about this issue. If you do research, remember to investigate both sides of the argument.

Now it's over to you to do some research

Here are four more animal issues:

Should animals be...

... used to entertain, for example, in a circus?

... kept in zoos?

... hunted for sport?

... kept as pets?

Task 6

1 With a partner, draw up a list of arguments **for** and **against** each issue. You can get ideas from your work on pages 106 and 107. You might need to do some more research of your own. Record your conclusions in a chart like this

Dilemma	Arguments for	Arguments against	My opinion

2 Which dilemma did you find the easiest to make up your mind about and which the hardest?

Final task

So ... is it right to eat animals?

Part One

Prepare a group presentation to include:

- a clear statement of the group's response to the question (it's OK to say you disagreed in your group as long as you say why!)
- a variety of opinions
- reasons that show you have read your notes.

Start with a clear statement of your group's opinion. Use quotations to back up your opinion:

We think that it is/is not OK to eat animals.

We think that the best reason for being a vegetarian is…

We think that the best reason for not being a vegetarian is…

We think that the most important reason why some religious people are vegetarian is…

Part Two

Prepare your personal response.

Write down your feelings and beliefs on an issue that you have thought about in this unit (for example, factory farming, vegetarianism, Hindu beliefs, vivisection). Your response could be in the form of a written paragraph, meditation, poem or prayer.

Bhaktivedanta Manor in Hertfordshire is a college for students who wish to devote their lives to the service and lifestyle of Lord Krishna.

Hindus believe that God (Brahman) may be worshipped in many forms. Three main forms are the deities Brahma (the creator), Vishnu (the preserver) and Shiva (the destroyer). Many Hindus in Britain focus their worship on Vishnu.

Hindus believe that when there is trouble in the world, Vishnu enters the world as an animal or human to save it. Vishnu once appeared as the human Krishna (see page 15).

Krishna is very popular among Hindus. He is thought of as loving and good. He is also well known as Govinda (a herder of cows) because he worked with cows, and protected and valued them greatly.

Vishnu appears, resting on the great serpent Ananta, floating on the cosmic ocean. From his navel comes Brahma, the creator.

Krishna surrounded by cows.

In 1983, the first 'cow protection scheme' in Europe was started at Bhaktivedanta Manor in Hertfordshire. It is a scheme of vegetarian, non-violent farming of cows and bulls. The animals are looked after until they die naturally. This means that only small numbers of cattle can be kept on the farm. There are, on average, fourteen cows and ten bulls on the farm.

Fields being harvested in the old-fashioned way.

The scheme encourages others to support the care of cows.

ESSENTIAL PRINCIPLES
OF
VEGETARIAN COW HUSBANDRY

1. Cows and Bulls must NOT be killed under any circumstance.

2. Calves MUST be allowed to suckle directly from their mother's udder until their natural weaning age of 7-10 months.

3. Cows MUST be hand-milked.

4. Bulls not engaged in a breeding programme should be trained in a respectful manner and their abilities utilised in a meaningful way. (e.g ploughing.)

5. Cows and bulls should be fed only natural vegetation - grasses, grains and suitable vegetables.

Rules of vegetarian cow husbandry.

The cows are milked and the bulls are given suitable work, such as pulling the carts for visiting school groups. Working the animals is good for them and means that the farm can keep going.

After the cows have been milked, they are brushed down and stroked. The herdsman tries to develop a loving and trusting relationship with the cows. Each cow is more contented and gives more milk.

Cattle have a special place of honour in the Hindu religion: the cow is respected because she gives milk like a natural mother; the bull is respected, as a father, because he ploughs the land producing grains and vegetables.

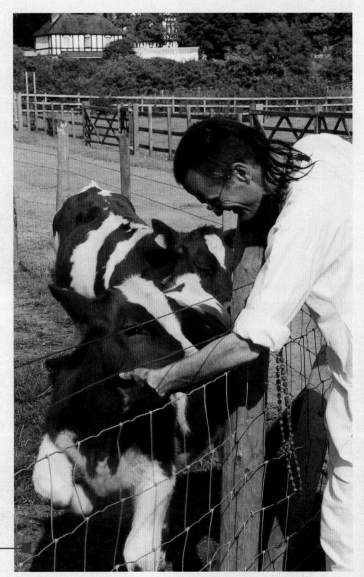

The cows are loved and a fuss is made of them!

Task

1 Below is a list of statements about cows.
Which ones would the students at Bhaktivedanta Manor agree with/disagree with?
Sort them into a table with two columns:

Would agree	Would not agree

- Modern machinery has helped a lot with working with cows.
- There is one eternal and universal Law. Part of that law is Ahimsa, non-violence.
- Once a bull is of no further use for breeding, there's no point in keeping it alive.
- Cows are sacred. Caring for and loving them brings us closer to God.
- To kill a cow would be like murder.
- When a cow produces no more milk, she can be slaughtered.
- Cows meet so many human needs: nourishment from milk, fuel and heat from dung.
- Modern farming methods are cruel. The animals are not given a chance to live – and die – naturally.

2 Imagine you are preparing for a school trip to Bhaktivedanta Manor. What would you want to ask about this project? Make a list of your questions.

The cows benefit from a lot of attention.

The farm is run according to Hindu principles.

9 The big picture

The Publishers of this book want to add an extra picture to the cover. They want an interesting picture but one which also shows the importance and value of religion.

A

B

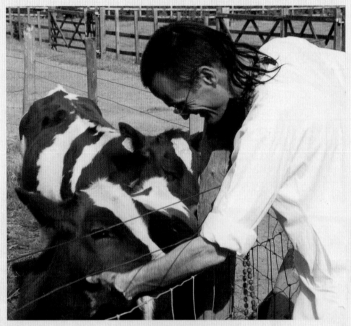

C

D

E

F

These are the six images that have been shortlisted. As users of the book, you have been asked for your point of view.

Task

1 Flip back through this book and write one sentence to explain what each of these six pictures is showing.
2 With a partner, decide which picture would be best for the book cover. Write down your reasons why this particular picture shows the importance and value of religions.
3 Hold a class vote to find the most popular choice.
4 Prepare an e-mail to the Publishers letting them know your choice and your reasons. It should start like this:

> I think that the best image for the front cover of this book would be . . .
> These are my three most important reasons:
> a)
> b)
> c)
> Signed ....

Glossary

AGNOSTIC   A person who doubts the existence of God

AHIMSA   Hindu belief that everything is sacred so there should be no killing or violence; respect for life

ANATTA   Buddhist belief that there is no unchanging, permanent self or soul in anybody or anything

ANICCA   Buddhist belief that everything is always changing; nothing or no one stays the same

APARTHEID   A system of government which separates people on the basis of racial difference

ARGUMENT   A reason to support a point of view

ATHEIST   A person who does not believe in the existence of God

BCE   Before Common Era; this is a neutral term to replace the traditional BC (Before Christ)

BELIEF   Something you know to be true or real, even though you can't always prove it to others; religious faith

BRAHMAN   Hindu name for the One Supreme Spirit at the heart of the universe, in everything and everyone

BUDDHA   A title meaning the Enlightened One; given to Siddattha Gotama, founder of Buddhism

CE   Common Era; this is a neutral term to replace the traditional AD (Anno Domini)

CONSULT   To ask for someone's opinion

CREATION   How something begins, for example, creation stories explain the beginning of the world and human life

CRUCIFIXION   Roman form of execution, used on Jesus (*v.* CRUCIFY)

DHAMMA   The teachings of Buddha

DHAMMACHAKRA   Symbol of Buddhism – a circle with eight sections representing the Eightfold Path

DHAMMAPADA   Buddhist collection of teachings

DUKKHA   Buddhist belief that life is unsatisfactory

EIGHTFOLD PATH   The Buddha's teaching on the way to live so that a person can get rid of greed, hatred and ignorance; the way to reach Nirvana

ENLIGHTENMENT   An understanding about what is true and real (see BUDDHA)

EXPERIENCE   Something that has happened to you; something felt or seen

FIVE PRECEPTS   Buddhist guidance about ways to become a better person

FOUR NOBLE TRUTHS   Teachings about change and suffering in life

INCARNATION   The Christian belief that God entered the world in the human form of Jesus

INTERDEPENDENCE   The recognition that human beings and the environment are connected and in need of each other

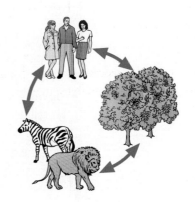

JESUS   Christians believe he was the son of God, sent to Earth to save people. His followers became the first Christians

JUSTICE   What is right and fair for everyone

KRISHNA In Hinduism, a very popular human form of Vishnu. He came to earth to overcome evil and bring goodness and love

KSHATRIYA A social class of kings and warriors (in India)

LEVITE A priest's assistant from Biblical times

MANDIR The name for the temple in which Hindus come together to worship

MEDITATION Thinking about something deeply; reflecting (*v.* MEDITATE)

MORAL DILEMMA A situation in which it is difficult to know what is right and wrong

MURTI The form or image used as a focal point in Hindu worship, for example, Krishna

NEIGHBOUR In the Christian story of the Good Samaritan, a neighbour means someone for whom you show consideration and care

NEW TESTAMENT A collection of 27 books making up the second part of the Christian Bible. The Old Testament, a collection of 39 books, makes up the first part of the Christian Bible and is also part of Jewish sacred writings

NIRVANA A word used by Buddhists to describe their goal – a state of true happiness, wisdom and peace. It is reached by the blowing out of the fires of greed, hatred and ignorance

OPINION A point of view, not necessarily shared by others

PARABLE A story told by Jesus to illustrate an ideal way of behaving

POLLUTION The contamination or spoiling of something, for example in the environment

PUJA   In Hindu worship, a Puja tray contains elements to focus the mind on worship, in the home or mandir

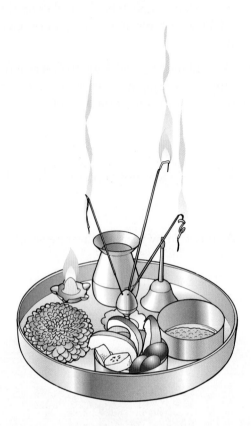

RECONCILIATION   The bringing together of people who have been enemies or set apart from each other

REINCARNATION   The Hindu belief that the soul is continually reborn in different forms. The form of a new existence is based on good or bad actions in a previous existence

RELIGION   A belief in the existence of a superhuman controlling power. This belief can be shown in different ways, which is why there are different religions. BUT, Buddhism does not believe in this superhuman power. Usually a religion has founders or leaders, sacred writings and ways of worshipping.

RENUNCIATION   Giving something up, for example, a certain way of life

RESURRECTION   The Christian belief that Jesus rose from the dead

RITUAL   Something which is done regularly, for example, in religious worship

SACRED   Something which is very special, respected and holy, such as sacred writings in religion. It can also be used in a non-religious way, as in the Earth is sacred

SAMARITAN   A native of Samaria. In Jesus' time, Samaritans and Jews hated each other

SANGHA   The community of Buddhists

SHRINE   The focal point for worship in some religions. In Hinduism it contains MURTIS

STEWARDSHIP   The responsibility of caring for the Earth

THEIST   A person who believes there is a God

THREE JEWELS   For Buddhists, these are the three very precious treasures: the Buddha, the Dhamma and the Sangha

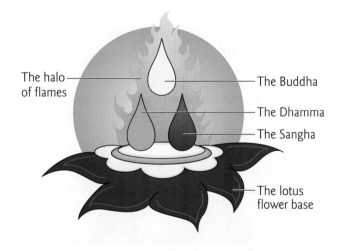

The halo of flames — The Buddha — The Dhamma — The Sangha — The lotus flower base

VEGETARIAN   A person who does not eat meat, fish or any product of animal slaughter. A vegan also excludes eggs, milk, cheese and all other animal products from his/her diet

VIVISECTION   The practice of performing experiments on animals, usually for medical research

Index

Acknowledgements

Written sources

p.59 Sally Humble-Jackson, *The Life of the Buddha*, 2000, with thanks to 4Learning; **p.75** Maurice Lynch, 'Kisagotami and her Baby'; **p.85** Sally Burns and Georgeanne Lamont, *Values and Visions* (adapted), Hodder and Stoughton Educational, 1996; **p.90** Olaf Skarsholt, 'If the Earth were small', 1990; **p.98** Angela Wood, 'Nothing and Everything' from *Creation Stories*, with thanks to 4Learning; **p.100** Edwin Brock, 'Song of the Battery Hen' from *And Another Thing*, Enitharmon Press, 1999.

Photo credits

Cover *background* Mauro Farmariello/Science Photo Library; **insets**: *t* © Ann & Bury Peerless, *c* Vivant Univers Photo Service, Belgium, *b* Peter Sanders; **p.4** *t* Space Telescope Science Institute/Science Photo Library, *b* © Lisa Woollett/Format; **p.5** *t* Peter Sanders, *b* CIRCA Photo Library/Robyn Beeche; **p.12** *t* CIRCA Photo Library/John Smith, *b* Peter Sanders; **p.13** CIRCA Photo Library/John Smith; **p.14** Peter Sanders; **p.16** *t* Robin Scagell/Science Photo Library, *b* Giraudon/Bridgeman Art Library; **p.17** NASA/Science Photo Library; **p.18** *tl* CIRCA Photo Library/Bipiri Mistry, *tr* © Dinesh Khanna/Axiom, *b* CIRCA Photo Library/John Smith; **p.19** *l* CIRCA Photo Library/John Smith, *r* © Chris Lisle/Corbis; **p.20** *tl & br* Shaun Botterill/Getty Images, *tr* Laurence Griffiths/Getty Images, *bl* Action Images/Darren Walsh; **p.21** *tl* David Leah/Getty Images, *tr & b* Sporting Pictures; **p.22** CIRCA Photo Library; **p.26** © J. Muafangeja Trust; **p.28** © National Gallery Picture Library; **p.31** Vivant Univers Photo Service, Belgium; **p.32-3** John Crook; **p.37** *t* Marcelo Brodsky/Science Photo Library, *bl* Tim Hetherington/CAFOD, *br* © Joanne O'Brien/Format; **p.51** *tl* © Paula Solloway/Format, *tr* © Joanne O'Brien/Format, *bl* © Jenny Matthews/Format, *br* © David & Peter Turnley/Corbis; **p.52** © David & Peter Turnley/Corbis; **p.54** © Ann & Bury Peerless; **p.58** Rabindra Kaur Singh, Twinstudio, UK (twinstudio@hotmail.com); **p.60** CIRCA Photo Library; **p.61** © Ted Streshinsky/Corbis; **p.64** CIRCA Photo Library/William Holtby; **p.68** Ann & Bury Peerless; **p.69** *all* Cath Large; **p.70** Cath Large; **p.76** Cath Large; **p.77** *both* Cath Large; **p.79** BSIP, Laurent/Science Photo Library; **p.80** CIRCA/William Holtby; **p.83** *tl & b* Cath Large, *tr* CIRCA/William Holtby; **p.84** NASA/Science Photo Library; **p.86** Peter Menzel/Science Photo Library; **p.87** Simon Fraser/Nothumbrian Environmental Management Ltd/Science Photo Library; **p.94** Rod Johnson/Link; **p.96** Simon Fraser/Nothumbrian Environmental Management Ltd/Science Photo Library; **p.98** © J. Muafangeja Trust; **p.99** © The British Museum, London; **p.101** George Lepp/Science Photo Library; **p.103** © Mo Wilson/Format; **p.106** © Richard T. Nowitz/Corbis; **p.107** Biomedical Research Education Trust; **p.108** *tl* © Maggie Murray/Format, *tr* © Bettmann/Corbis, *bl* © Brenda Prince/Format, *br* © Rebecca Peters/Format; **p.109** *t* © Richard T. Nowitz/Corbis, *ct* Biomedical Research Education Trust, *cb* © Maggie Murray/Format, *b* © Mo Wilson/Format; **p.110** *t* © The British Museum, London, *b* © Ananta Sakti; **p.111** *both* Cath Large; **p.112** *t* from 'Protecting Cows' by Syamasundara Hasa, Hatagra Publishing, Hove, Sussex, *b* Cath Large; **p.113** *both* Cath Large; **p.114** *tl* Giraudon/Bridgeman Art Library, *tr* Cath Large; **p.115** *l* Cath Large, *r* NASA/Science Photo Library; **p.116** © Ann & Bury Peerless; **p.117** *t* © Ananta Sakti, *b* Simon Fraser/Nothumbrian Environmental Management Ltd/Science Photo Library.

b = bottom, *c* = centre, *l* = left, *r* = right, *t* = top.

Every effort has been made to trace all copyright holders, but if any have been inadvertently overlooked the Publishers will be pleased to make the necessary arrangements at the first opportunity.